Reignbeau's

Riddles and Rhymes

by

Reignbeau the Clown

"Until Heaven and Earth pass away
... until it all comes true." (Mt 5:18)

What did the acquitted murder suspect say? "No noose is good noose."

What did the tuba call his father? Oom-papa.

What do you call a saint with bare feet, thin limbs, visions and bad breath? Super-calloused, fragile mystic who has halitosis.

Why can't a biped gallop? It doesn't have forelegs.

When an elevator not an elevator? When it's going down.

What do you get when you cross a crocodile and an abalone. Acrocabalone.

What do you get when you cross a frog with a shaggy dog? A croaker spaniel.

What do you get when you cross a pointer and an Irish setter? A poinsetter.

What do you get when you cross a small horn and a flute? A tooty flutey.

What's greenish, has a trunk and its head between its legs? A seasick traveler.

What happened to the bird who backed into the fan? It came out shredded tweet.

Have you read the new book on levitation? I couldn't put it down!

What happened to the couple who tried to kiss in the fog? They mist.

What did the fisherman say to his wife? Not tonight, I have a haddock.

When did a dozen cops chase one criminal? 12:48, twelve to one.

What's the difference between a psychologist and a magician? A magician pulls rabbits out of hats and a psychologist pulls habits out of rats!

What do you get when you cross a water lily and a kidney bean? A plant that waters itself.

Why is a cyberkiss like a straw hat? They're not felt.

What do you call it when you're half-afraid? Twotitude.

Knock! Knock! Who's there? **Señor.** Señor who? **Señor for sale sign and want to buy your house.**

What do you get when you cross a chef with a rooster? A Cook-a-doodle-doo.

What has eighteen legs and red spots and catches flies? A baseball team with measles.

Why was 6 afraid of 7? 7 ate 9.

Knock! Knock! Who's there? **Dozen.** Dozen who? **Dozen anyone in there know me?**

Which of Arthur's knights tended to the wounded? Sir Geon.

What happened to 288? I can't say; it's too gross!

What do you get when you cross a mink and a boa? A coat that eats goats.

Knock! Knock! Who's there? **Wendy.** Wendy who? **Wendy saints go marching in ...**

What's the difference between a gossip and a comedian? One spreads rumor, the other humor.

How many Scotsmen does it take to change a light bulb? None, because it's cheaper to sit in the dark.

What happened to the man who fell into a vat of root beer? Nothing; it was a soft drink.

How's the man who had his left side amputated? He's all right now.

Have you read the mew book on improving your memory? I think so.

What happened to the engaged man with a wooden leg? Her father broke it off.

What's large, gray and wears glass slippers? Cinderell-ephant.

What did the chemist name his daughter? Ann Eliza.

What do you call a small, insignificant elephant? Irrel-ephant

What has 400 teeth and says "Beware of the dog." A picket fence with a sign on it.

What is wrinkled, gray, and young? A baby elephant.

What is wrinkled, purple and from Denmark? A prune Danish.

What's green, bumpy and always changing? A fickle pickle.

What's better than being forthright and honest? Fifthright and honest.

What do you get if you cross a black widow and a horse? A poisonous spider you can ride to the hospital.

What is gray and blue all over? An elephant holding its breath.

Have you read the new book on paranoia? Why do you want to know!

What happened to the canary that pecked at the wall outlet? It got an electric bill.

What do you get if you cross the Atlantic with the *Titanic*? Part way.

What is green and blue all over? A pickle holding its breath.

What is orange and red all over? A sunburned carrot.

Have you read the new book on curing insomnia? I finished it at 5 a. m.!

What has eight legs, two arms and two wings? A bird on a man on horseback.

What has 18 legs and catches flies? A baseball team.

Why did the dog chain break? It was bound to a cur.

Have you read the new book on milk? I skimmed it.

What makes the Tower of Pisa lean? It does eat much.

What's Tarzan's favorite Christmas carol? Jungle Bells.

What's the difference between a weightlifting novice and a cookbook author? One has an aching back and the other's a baking hack.

How many country singers does it take to change a light bulb? Five, one to make the change and a backup quartet to sing about missing the old bulb.

Why'd the fool return the library book unread? He found out *How to Hug* was a volume of the encyclopedia.

Why is the tuba good for your mouth? A tuba toothpaste helps clean your teeth.

What did the chick join the marching band? It already had the drumsticks.

What has tentacles, lives in the ocean and kills? Billy the Squid.

What do elephants do for fun? Tell people jokes.

What's the best drink during a marathon? Running water.

Which of Arthur's knights made sure the Round Table was round? Sir Cular.

What do you get if you cross a sheep and a kangaroo? A sweater with pockets.

What has 44 legs and runs in two directions at once? Two football teams.

Name a couple of the largest rivers in the U. S.? The Mississippi. Right! **And the second?** The Mr. Sippy?

What has a hump and red spots? A camel with the measles.

What do you get if you cross a cocker spaniel, poodle and rooster? A Cockapoodledoo.

What is green and lives in the ocean? Moby pickle.

Knock! Knock! Who's there? **Henrietta.** Henrietta who? **Henrietta big lunch and isn't coming for supper.**

Knock! Knock! Who's there? **Juliet.** Juliet who? **Juliet with Henrietta, so she'snot coming either.**

What goes "Aab! Aab!" A sheep going backward.

What goes "Slam! Slam! Slam! Slam!" A four-door automobile.

What kind of bee can't make up its mind? A May bee.

What kind of coat is always put on wet? A coat of paint.

What is elephants' favorite sport? Squash.

Knock! Knock! Who's there? **Heywood Hugh.** Heywood Hugh who? **Heywood Hugh open the door soon?**

What kind of drink do kings and queens drink? Royal tea.

Knock! Knock! Who's there? **Juana?** Juana who? **Juana open the door now?**

What has twenty-two legs and makes crunching sounds? A football team eating chips.

What kind of geometrical figure's most correct? A right angle.

What kind of hawk has no wings? A tomahawk.

What's the new, improved Ford called? Fived.

How many thought police does it take to change a light bulb? None, because "There never was a light bulb."

What kind of illness can't you talk about until you're well? Laryngitis.

Have you read the new book on suicides? No, but I'm dying to.

What do you get if you cross an octopus with straw? An eight-handled broom.

What kind of room is always doorless and windowless? Mushroom.

What clothes are never worn out? Underwear.

What kind of running is walking? Running out of gas.

What's white, fluffy and lives in trees? A meringue-utang.

Knock! Knock! Who's there? **Phineas.** Phineas who? **Phineas thing happened on the way here. Wanna hear?**

What do you get if you cross a sponge and a potato? It doesn't taste so good, but it really soaks up the gravy.

What's red, hairless and has long fangs? A sabre-tooth apple.

What's large, gray and goes around and around and around? An elephant stuck in a revolving door.

Knock! Knock! Who's there? **Judah.** Judah who? **Judah known by now, if you'd just opened the door.**

What's the difference between a duck and a football player? One goes into a puddle, the other a huddle.

What would you call a raisin's mother's mother? A grape grandmother.

Which of Arthur's knight was immortalized as a statue? Sir Ramic.

What'd you call 25 score Native Americans without apples? The Indian apple-less 500.

What did Dela wear? A brand new jersey.

What's six-foot long, green and has two tongues? The Green Giant's sneakers.

What's the difference between a dog and a marine biologist? One wags a tail, the other tags a whale.

What's the difference between a dressmaker and a baseball pitcher? One seeks wins, the other sequins.

What's the difference between a dressmaker and a nurse? One cuts dresses, the other dresses cuts.

What's the difference between a dry-docked ship and a driver in the fog? One can't go to sea, the other can't see to go.

How many Calvinists does it take to change a light bulb? None, because God has already predestined which are going to change.

What you get if you cast demons into swine? Deviled ham.

Have you read the book on the *Titanic*? Fortunately no!

Molecule to ion: **"Are you sure you lost an electron?"** Ion to molecule: **"I'm positive!"**

What do you call a person who jumps off a Paris bridge? In Seine.

How did furrows Connecti cut? With an Ida hoe.

What's purple, wrinkled and hops? A prune on a pogo stick.

Why didn't the grape scream when he got smashed? Because all it could do was let out a
little wine.

Why'd the bachelor marry an electrician's daughter? She sparked his interest.

How many professors does it take to change a light bulb? None, that's what grad
students are for.

What good's a reindeer? It helps the flowers grow, sweetie.

Neutron to Bartender: **"How much do I owe you?"** Bartender to neutron: **"For you -- no
charge."**

What shameful thing did Tennes see? The same as Arkan saw, Wiscon sin.

Will February march? No, but April may.

Why didn't the elephant cross the road? So as not to be mistaken for a chicken.

Why don't you want an electric toothbrush? Because you don't have any electric teeth.

What's the difference between a prison guard and someone with measles? One spots
outbreaks and the other breaks out in spots.

Why didn't the frog jump for joy? It was too unhoppy.

Have you read the new book on palindromes? Did I? I did.

When is a greeting not a greeting? When it's a hoy.

What's the difference between an elephant and peanut butter? An elephant won't stick
to the roof of your mouth.

Why'd the bachelor marry the stonecutter's daughter? She did't take him for granite.

How many actors does it take to change a stagelight? Two, one to climb up on stage and
do it and one to say, "I wish I were up there."

Why didn't the guru with a toothache go to the dentist? He wanted to transcend dental medication.

Knock! Knock! Who's there? **Pavlov.** You rang?

Waiter, I asked for new mustard! This is the same! waiter: **It's Dijon Vu.**

Why did the farmer get rid of his milk cow? She was an udder failure.

Which of Arthur's knights was the smartest? Sir Rebral.

Why did the golfer carry an extra sock? In case he got a hole in one.

Knock! Knock! Who's there? **Jenny.** Jenny who? **Jenny'd any help opening the door?**

What's the definition of 'shotgun wedding". A case of wife or death.

Knock! Knock! Who's there? **Goliath.** Goliath who? **Goliath down. You sound tired.**

Why doesn't anyone ever counterfeit pennies? That'd be non-cents!

Why is a good pitcher like a good cook? They both know their batters.

What word is most often pronounced erroneously? Erroneously.

Knock! Knock! Who's there? **Harvey.** Harvey who? **Harvey going to keep this up all night?**

Why is good pitcher like a good piano tuner? They both have perfect pitch.

Why'd the bachelor marry the dockworker's daughter? She had no peer.

What happened when the goat ate the broken window? It got a pane in the stomach.

Have you read the new book on waterfowl anatomy? Do ducks have lips?

Why is a stadium always hotter after a game? The fans are all gone.

Knock! Knock! Who's there? **Kenya.** Kenya who? **Kenya open the door, please?**

Why is doing nothing so exhausting? You can never stop to rest.

What's the name of the carpenter union's brass quartet? The Tuba Four.

Why is it difficult to recognize cattle from the rear? They're always switching their tails.

Knock! Knock! Who's there? **Hans.** Hans who. **Hans up! This is a burglary.**

Why was the professional chess player happy? He could take a knight off.

Why'd the bachelor marry a farmer's daughter? She'd was outstanding in her field.

How can you tell if an elephant has been in your frig? Elephant prints in the butter.

What's the difference between a skillet and a celebrity stalker? One's a frying pan and the other's a prying fan.

Knock! Knock! Who's there? **Arthur.** Arthur who? **Arthuritis keeping from opening the door?**

What happened to the judge that got the awful farm boundary dispute? A my-grain headache.

Why'd the bachelor marry cabby's daughter? He'd always wanted to meet her.

What's the difference between pride and vanity? Pride is what we have; vanity is what other's have.

Why were the belt and suspenders arrested? For holding up pants.

Why would you want holes in your socks? To put your feet in.

Which of Arthur's knights was always right? Sir Tain.

How are stars like false teeth? They both come out at night.

Knock! Knock! Who's there? **Ivan.** Ivan who? **Ivan idea, why don't you let me in?**

What's the commonest use for cowhide. Covering cows.

How do chicken prepare every meal? From scratch.

What can you add to a bottle of beer to make it lighter? A hole.

Have you read the new book on improving decision-making skills? Should I?

What's the definition of "lottery"? A tax on those who don't understand probability.

What's the best way to cook a ten-foot python? Use shortening.

How can you keep a wild rhino from charging? Take away its credit cards.

How do you make a lemon drop? First you pick it up, then you let it go.

How can you make a slow horse fast? Stop feeding it.

Why'd the bachelor marry the optician's daught? She never made a spectacle of herself.

What did the engineer name his daughter? Bridget.

Your wife was a milkman's daughter? Yes, but she was the cream of the crop.

What's the easiest way to get rid of varnish? Remove the R.

How do you hide in a camel herd? Camelflage.

If a papa bull eats three bales a day and a baby bull eats one, what's a mama bull eat? Nothing, because there's no such thing as a mama bull.

Knock! Knock! Who's there? **Gunnar.** Gunnar who? **Gunnar huff and puff, if you don't open this door.**

What's the cause of male pattern baldness? Lack of hair.

What's white and fluffy and swings from trees? A meringue-utan.

What's adversary in three letters, not FOE? NME (enemy).

What's covetousness in two letters? NV (envy).

Have you read the new book on phobias? I'm afraid not.

Knock! Knock! Who's there? **Edward.** Edward who? **Edward B. nice if you'd open the door.**

What's evacuated in two letters? MT (empty).

Why'd the bachelor marry the camper's daughter? Her devotion was intense.

What's super-sagacious in two letters? YY (too wise).

Knock! Knock! Who's there? **Eisenhower.** Eisenhower who? **Eisenhower late; forgive me?**

What's the difference between a bully and an ice cream cone? One licks you and the other you lick.

Knock! Knock! Who's there? **Howard.** Howard who? **Howard I. know.**

What's the difference between a play and a recital? Performers recite at a play and play at a recital.

What's the difference between Caesar's barber and a sideshow huckster? One's shaving a Roman, the other's a raving showman.

What's the difference between a cheetah and a duck? One goes quick, the other "Quack!"

What's the difference between a composer and a church historian? One writes notes, the other notes rites.

Your wife was a florist's daughter? Yes, but she had the most beautiful tulips.

Which of Arthur's knights was most like a snake? Sir Pentine.

Who's the most famous male elephant singer? Harry Elephante.

Knock! Knock! Who's there? **Babylon.** Babylon who? **Babylon if you want; just open the door.**

What's the difference between a legume farmer and an Broadway actor? One minds his peas, the other his cues.

Who's the most famous female elephant singer? Elephants' Gerald.

What's the difference between a crooked politician and church bell? One steals from the people, the other peals from the steeple.

Knock! Knock! Who's there? **Barbie.** Barbie who? **Barbie Q. Chicken.**

What's the difference between a dog and a gossip? One has a wagging tail, the other a wagging tongue.

Why'd the bachelor marry the plumber's daughter? She gave his heart a wrench.

Who're only successful when they're down and out? Astronauts and cosmonauts.

What do you get if you cross a rhino with a goose? A big animal that honks before it runs over you.

Why are tall people lazier than short ones? They're always longer in bed.

Knock! Knock! Who's there? **Archer.** Archer who? **Archer glad to see me?**

Your wife was a prospector's daughter? Yes, but she had a mine of her own.

How many agnostics does it take to change a light bulb? None, because they can't tell the darkness from the Light.

Knock! Knock! Who's there? **I. B. Long.** I. B. Long who? **I. B. Long inside, so open the door.**

What didn't the tortoise race the cat? It was a cheetah.

Why did the Alaskan island disappear? It was an optical Aleutian.

Why did the banana go out with a prune? Because it couldn't get a date.

What's the difference between a covered wagon and a threatening gardener? One's a prairie schooner and the other a scary pruner.

How'd the silkworm race end up? In a tie.

Why did the baker fail at growing oranges? Bakers can't be juicers.

Why do birds fly south for the winter? It's too far to walk.

Why did the clock have to leave the library? It tocked too loud.

Knock! Knock! Who's there? **Belle Lee.** Belle Lee who? **Belle Lee, dancer.**

Why did the house need a doctor? It had window panes.

What did the dog owner name the pup born in the melon patch? Melon collie baby.

Why did the whale cross the ocean? To get to the other tide.

Knock! Knock! Who's there? **Andy Greene.** Andy Greene who? **Andy Greene grass grew all around...**

What did the homeowner tell the painters? Repaint and thin no more.

What did the cat say to the elephant? Meow.

Which cat ate the Czech lion-tamer, the lioness or the lion? The Czech's in the male.

Knock! Knock! Who's there? **Cargo.** Cargo who? **No, cargo "Vroom!"; owl go "Who!"**

Why did the otter cross the road? To get to the otter side.

Which letters are the most jealous? Jealous C and jealous E.

What

Knock! Knock! Who's there? **Frank Lee.** Frank Lee who? **Frank Lee I don't believe you want to open the door.**

Why did the ram walk over the cliff? He didn't see the ewe turn.

Why did the rich man refuse a local anesthetic? He would only accept imported.

What happened to the lightning bug that backed into a fan? It was de-lighted.

Where has Ore gone? Where Massachu sets.

Why did the house need a doctor? It had window pains.

How do you unlock a Kentuc? With a Kentuc key?

Knock! Knock! Who's there? **Danielle.** Danielle who? **Danielle. I can hear you.**

How much did Yei owe Ming? The price of a minisoda?

What did the carpet say to the floor? Don't move! I've got you covered!

Why'd the bachelor marry the prospector's daughter? She had a mind of her own.

Who did Ill annoy? Merry Land, because he rode Island.

What happens when spoons are overworked? They go stir crazy.

What's the difference between an elephant and a flea? An elephant can have fleas, but a flea can't have elephants.

Why couldn't the blonde use her box seat? She'd already used the bleachers.

What's the difference between a fisherman and a sinner? One baits the hook, the other hates the Book.

Did they catch that midget fortuneteller yet? No, the small medium's at large.

What's the difference between a groundskeeper and a launderer? One keeps the lawn wet, the other the laundry.

Why does the toast like the knife? It buttered him up.

Why did the strawberry need a lawyer? It got itself into a jam.

Knock! Knock! Who's there? **Don.** Don who? **Don' ask questions; jus' open the door.**

What's the difference between a good driver and a bad one? W, one is wreckless, the other reckless.

What did the police do with the burger burgler? The grilled him.

Why is it dangerous to make a witch angry? She'll fly off her broom handle.

What's the difference between a gossip and a mirror? One speaks without reflecting, the other reflects without speaking.

What's the difference between a hen and a rooster? When one eats chickenfeed, she's eating; when the other is he is.

What's the difference between hill and a pill? One's hard to get up, the other to get down.

Why was the water fountain arrested? For being drunk in public.

Why couldn't the monkey find a banana? The banana split.

What do you call heretics who hate Superman? Lexluthorans.

What's big, likes peanuts and has a trunk? A tree with a squirrel in it.

What do you get if you cross a cat and a lemon? A sourpuss.

What's the difference between a lion with a toothache and a storm cloud? One roars with pain, the other pours with rain.

If two's company and three's a crowd, what're four and five? Nine.

What has 5 legs, 3 eyes, and 2 trunks? An elephant with spare parts.

What's the difference between Caesar's barber and a sideshow huckster? One's shaving a Roman, the other's a raving showman.

What's the difference between a judge and an icemaker? One dispenses justice, the other just ice.

Why'd the bachelor marry the preacher's daughter? You couldn't put anything past her.

What's the difference between someone walking upstairs and someone just watching them? One steps up the stairs, the other stares up the steps.

What do you get if you cross a duck and a firefly? A firequaker.

What's the difference between a New Yorker and a dentist? One roots for the Yanks, the other yanks for the roots.

What do you get if you cross a dog and an alligator? A very wary mail carrier.

How many Catholics does it take to change a light bulb? None, they use candles.

Knock! Knock! Who's there? **Giovanni.** Giovanni who? **Giovanni come out to play?**

What's the difference between a parrot and a duck hunter? One wants a cracker, the other a quacker.

Why do umpires have good appetites? They always clean their plates.

Which of Arthur's knights had the most energy? Sir Charged.

What's the difference between a racehorse and a locomotive? One's trained to run, the other runs the train.

What's the difference between a scale and a hammer? One can weigh a pound, the other can pound away.

When is water unfreezable? When boiling.

What's the difference between a shepherd and bloodhound? One knows his ewes, the other uses his nose.

What do you get if you cross a Romanoff with a fish? A czardine.

What's the difference between the jungle and a pizzeria? One has a man-eating tiger, the other a man eating pizza.

Why do you find frogs in the outfield? They're good at catching flies.

What's the difference between the beach and the letter D? One's before the sea, the other after the C.

What do you get if you cross a cactus with a bicycle? A flat tire.

What's the difference between the sun and a loaf of bread? One rises from the east, the other from the yeast.

What's worse than a giraffe with a sore throat? A centipede with sore feet.

How many aerospace engineers does it take to change a light bulb? None, after all it's not rocket science.

What's worse than it raining cats and dogs? Hailing taxis.

When does happiness come before heaven? In the dictionary.

Why'd the bachelor marry the wrestler's daughter? She alway came through in the clinch.

Where would you find a ruler just three foot tall? At a yard sale.

Where's the ocean the deepest? On the bottom.

If a snake hides under a small rock when it's sunny, what kind does it hide under when it's raining? A wet one.

What's the difference between democracy and feudalism? In one your vote counts and in the other your count votes.

Why would an elephant paint its toenails red. To hide in the strawberry patch.

What do you call a nearly silent bee? A mumblebee.

What do you call a calf after it's six months old? Seven months old.

What do you call a knife that can cut four loaves at once? A four-loaf cleaver.

Knock! Knock! Who's there? **Heaven.** Heaven who? **heaven you recognized me yet?**

What do you call the two hundred year anniversary of Buffalo? The Bison-tennial.

What do you call a man born in Greece, raised in Spain, moved to America and then died in Mexico? Dead.

What do you call someone who builds gates for alleys? An alley-gater.

What's green, edible and many eyes? A potatoad.

How would a frog build a skyscraper? Rivet, rivet, rivet.

What does Lancelot wear to bed? A knight shirt.

Why couldn't the fool get his snow tires to work? They melted.

What happened to the boy who ran away with the circus? The police made him return it.

What is black when bought, red when used and gray after it's used? Coal.

What eats more without a bit in its mouth? A horse.

What gets wetter as it dries? A towel.

Knock! Knock! Who's there? **Freddy.** Freddy who? **Freddy or not here I am.**

Why was six afraid of seven? Because seven ate nine.

What can run along miles of road and never move? A fence.

What grows down as it grows up? A duck or goose.

What has a neck but not head and arms but not legs? A shirt.

When does December come before November? In the dictionary. **What has eight legs and sings?** A barbershop quartet.

What has fifty heads and fifty tails but no legs? A roll of pennies.

What is it that stays stationary even when everything else is going up in price? Writing paper and envelopes.

Knock! Knock! Who's there? **Radio.** Radio who? **Radio not, here I come!**

What has many eyes but cannot see? A potato.

How can you tell if an elephant's under your bed? If it was you'd be squashed up against the ceiling.

When does December come before January? When the year changes.

Why'd the bachelor marry printer's daughter? She was just his type.

What's bought by the yard, but worn by the foot? A carpet.

What is brought to the table and cut but never eaten? A deck of cards.

What's purple and over 5,000 miles long? The Grape Wall of China.

What is filled every day and emptied every night, except once a year? A stocking.

Why do elephants have gray skin? To keep their insides together.

What is it that runs but can't walk? Water.

What is harder to catch the faster you run? Your breath.

What is it that makes men mean? Not their testosterone, but the letter A.

What is large at the bottom, small at the top and has many eers? A mountain.

What is longer if you cut off from either end? A ditch.

What should you do if you find a blue elephant? Cheer it up.

When does April come before March? In the dictionary.

What is it that is older than its legs? A frog.

Why must God the Father be left-handed? Because Jesus sits on his right.

What is taller sitting than standing? A dog.

Why'd the bachelor marry the communist's daughter? She was classy.

What keeps out bugs and shows movies? A screen.

What wears shoes but has no feet? A sidewalk.

What takes many steps to go up and down yet never moves? Stairs.

If six won twice why was it disappointed? Because zero won too, three for five.

What is it that talks a lot and lives in the Himalayas? A yakety yak.

How many paleontologists does it take to change a light bulb? Three, one to find it and two others to disagree over how old it is.

What do you throw away the outside of, cook the inside of, eat the outside of and throw away the inside? Corn on the cob.

Where can you find flat mountains and dry oceans? On a map.

What was made many years ago, yet is made again daily? A bed.

What was made many years ago, yet is new every month? The moon.

What has one eye and no legs, yet moves like the wind? A hurricane.

What wears a coat all year but pants only in the summer? A dog.

What kind of animal eats and drinks with its tail? All tailed ones do; they don't eat or drink without one. map

What kind of bird is the strongest? A crane.

What kind of clothes did Cinderella wear? Wish and wear.

Knock! Knock! Who's there? **Mae.** Mae who? **Mae be I'll tell you and maybe I won't.**

What kind of ant is the largest? A gi-ant.

Why is an eye like Jesus being scourged? Both ar under the lash.

Knock! Knock! Who's there? **Joe King.** Joe King who? Just Joe King with you.

What kind of table has no legs? A multiplication table.

What kind of tree do you find in a kitchen? A pan tree.

What's the best way to get down from an elephant? You don't get down from an elephant; you get down from a goose.

When doesn't January come before February? In the dictionary.

What makes a hearse horse hoarse? The coughin'.

What nationality are Santa's elves? North Polish.

What odd number can you take two from and make it even? Eleven.

What should you do if you find a yellow elephant? Encourage it.

What would you get if you crossed a bloodhound and a greyhound? A bloodhound that seats 45 passengers.

What did the hat say to the scarf? Hang around here for a while, while I go on a head.

When are the yellow pages not yellow? When they're read.

The alphabet has twenty-six letters; if you took one away how many would you have?

Still twenty-six, because 1 is a number not a letter.

Twenty-three, because "one" is a three-letter word.

Why'd the bachelor marry the tailor's daughter? She'd give you the shirt off his back.

How many babysitters does it take to change a light bulb? None, because they don't make diapers that small.

Knock! Knock! Who's there? **Justin.** Justin who? **Justin time to open the door.**

What would you get if you crossed a clock and a chicken? An alarm cluck.

What should you do if you find a white elephant? Hold its trunk until it turns blue. **And if it's blue?** Cheer it up.

What would you get if you crossed a dog and an egg? A pooched egg.

What would you get if you crossed a dog and a waffle? A woofle.

What's the cryogenicist's favorite song? "Freeze a Jolly Good Fellow".

Why couldn't the potato play ball? It was just a common tater.

What's green and sings? Elvis Parsley.

What did the doctor ask the injured gymnast? What's a bad joint like this doing in a nice girl like you?

What's green and toots? A pickle-o.

What's the Chinese restaurant's soupe du jour? It was tried and found Won Ton.

Why wouldn't the captain abandon his sinking ship? It was beneath him.

Why should poetry be an a labor of love? Rhyme does not pay.

What is the difference between a lemon and an elephant? A lemon's yellow.

Why'd the bachelor marry the streetcleaner's daughter? She swept him away.

What's left if you take half from a half dollar? A dollar.

What's orange, has large fangs and hangs from tree? A saber-tooth kumquat.

What's faster -- hot or cold? Hot, anyone can catch cold.

What's the difference between a seamstress and a stable hand? One mends a tear, the other tends a mare.

What did the judge tell the bigamist? You can't have you Kate and Esdith too.

Why was the vender nicknamed Napoleon? He mustard the franks.

Why don't elephants ride bicycles? They don't have thumbs to ring the bell.

How many divas does it take to change a light bulb? Just one to hold the light bulb while the world revolves around her.

What's green and pecks at trees? Woody Woodpickle.

What's the best cure for insomnia? A good night's sleep.

What did zero say to eight? Nice belt.

What's the difference between a Scot and a dog? One wears kilts and the other pants.

When's a river considered impassable? When it's too big for its bridges.

When'd Lancelot contemplate his navel? The middle of the knight.

How many entertainers does it take to change a light bulb? Ten -- one for the money, two for the show, three to get ready and four to go.

When doesn't morning come before afternoon? In the dictionary.

What's the difference between a train and a teacher? One says "Choo! Choo!" and the other "Don't chew! Don't chew!"

When does Christmas come before Thanksgiving. In the dictionary.

When is a black cat most likely to want to come in the house? When it's outside.

Why didn't the dyslexic atheist mail carrier believe he'd get bitten? He didn't believe in dog.

When is a chair like a fabric? When it's sat in.

What time is it when the clock strikes 13? Time to fix the clock.

When is July before June? In the dictionary.

When is longhand quicker than shorthand? On a clock.

When does Monday come before Sunday and Friday before Thursday? In the dictionary.

How many optimists does it take to change a light bulb? None, because they know it'll get brighter.

When is November before October and October before September? In the dictionary.

What would you call a great white whale that may not exist? Maybe Dick.

When is pocket change like the moon? When it's got four quarters.

Why'd the bachelor marry the mailcarrier's daughter? She handles the male with care.

Knock! Knock! Who's there? **X. Q.** X. Q. who? **X. Q.'s me; I must have the wrong address.**

Which burns longer the candles on a boy's birthday cake or those on a girl's? Neither, both burn shorter.

Where do chickens dance? A fowl ball.

When is the best time for using a trampoline? In Springtime.

Where does Lancelot dance? The knight club.

When does June come before May? In the dictionary.

Which of Arthur's knights didn't expect the ambush? Sir Prized.

Where do snowmen dance? A snow ball.

Where was the Declaration of Independence signed? At the bottom.

Where'd you go to learn the ice cream business? Sundae school.

Who is most likely to get struck by lightning if a band plays in a thunderstorm? The conductor.

Why didn't the baseball teams tie if no man ever touched base? They were all-girl teams.

What kind of cow can speak Russian? Ma's cow.

Knock! Knock! Who's there? **Li'l Ole Lady.** Li'l Ole Lady who? **I didn't kmow you could yodel!**

Which is better: "Your house burned down?" or "Your house burned up?" Both are bad!

Which is correct -- "29 plus 15 is 43." or "29 plus 15 are 43."? Neither, 29 plus 15 is 44.

Why didn't the dentist and the manicurist get married? They fought tooth and nail.

What was the name of the explorer to the cannibals? Stu.

Which school makes you drop out before you can graduate? Parachute school.

What is the difference between woman who knits and one who doesn't? One's a knitter and the other's not her.

Why didn't the one who borrowed the economics book returned to the library? He was a bookkeeper.

What did the alien say to the forest ranger? Take me to your cedar.

Which takes longer to run -- first base to second or second base to third? Second to third because there's a short stop in between.

Who's larger Mr. Bigger, Mrs. Bigger or their baby? The baby's a little Bigger.

Who makes up jokes about knitting? A knitwit.

Why don't carpenters build with stone? They never saw it.

Knock! Knock! Who's there? **Willoughby.** Willoughby who? **Willoughby my friend?**

How many apes does it take to change a light bulb? Many generations, until they evolve opposable thumbs.

What did the ocean to the shore? Nothing, it just waved.

Why don't fish smoke cigarettes? They don't want to get hooked.

Knock! Knock! Who's there? **Yul.** Yul who? **Yul never guess, so open the door.**

Why didn't the hourglass keep accurate time? It had quicksand in it.

Why didn't the orange cross the road? It ran out of juice.

Which side of a cow has more hair? The outside.

Why is Easter like tea? Easter and T both come at the end of Lent.

Which side of a pie is the left side? The side not yet eaten.

Why didn't the policeman ticket the truck driver going the wrong way down a one-way street? The truck driver was a pedestrian.

What do you call a ten-book series? A novelty.

Why didn't the bicycle go dancing? It was two-tired.

What kind of animal are you when you have a cold? A little horse.

What kind of animal are you when you take a shower? A little bear.

How do you catch a squirrel? Climb up a tree and act like a nut.

What did the poet call his overactive snake? A hyper viper.

How many carpenters does it take to change a light bulb? None, that's the electricians job.

Why didn't the tortoise race the cat? It was a cheetah.

Why is A like noon. They're both in the middle of day.

What do you call a decathlon athlete? Sportty.

Why didn't the vampire like Eurasians? He liked full-blooded Europeans or Asians.

Why do cowboys ride horses when out on the range? They're too heavy to carry.

Why do dragons sleep during the day? So they can fight knights.

Knock! Knock! Who's there? **Hu.** Hu who? **Quite an echo in there, isn't there?**

Were can you find werewolves? In a were-house.

Why do fish swim in schools? Because they can't walk.

Why do you go to bed at bedtime? Because the bed won't come to you.

Why did the bandage need a lawyer? It got ripped off.

Why does B come before C? Because one must be before one can see.

Why does the ocean sometimes become angry? Because it's been crossed so many times.

What's a cat's favorite color? Purrple.

What's a plumbers favorite shoes? Clogs.

Why didn't the weightlifter cross the road? The traffic was too heavy.

Why are cowboys confused by decimals? They never round down.

What's the difference between a tailor and a farmer? One sews rips and the other sows and reaps.

Knock! Knock! Who's there? **Watts.** Watts who? **Watts up, Doc?**

Why does St. Nicholas wear a beard? Because when he tries to shave, he Nicks himself.

When does August come before July? In the dictionary.

What didn't the cannibal eat the clown? It tasted funny.

Which of Arthur's knights died from liver damage? Sir Rhosis.

What's the difference between a hardware store and a software store? One sells windows and the other Windows.

When is it time for a doctor to retire? When he runs out of patients.

Knock! Knock! Who's there? **Cosmo.** Cosmo who? **Cosmo Stovus are still outside, why don't you let us in.**

What did the judge say to the skunk? Odor in the court!

Why did the dog re-cross the road? Trying to fetch a boomerang.

Why'd the cat frat move in next to the mouse house? So they could invite the neighbors for supper.

Why wouldn't it be right to get a car for a 15-year-old? It wouldn't be a fair trade.

What's the difference between a red light and a green light? The color!

What has one horn and gives milk? A milk truck.

How many economists does it take to change a light bulb? At least three in order to get a majority who agree on which way the light bulb is expected to turn.

How can Superman leap higher than a tall building? Because buildings can't leap at all.

Why isn't the human cannonball still at the circus? He was discharged.

Why isn't tissue paper used for writing on? Because it's so tearable.

Why was Cinderella no good at sports? She ran away from the ball.

Why do scientists always confirm their experimental results? Because it's called re-search.

Why was the baby raised on wild goat's milk? It was a wild kid.

When is a sailor not a sailor? When he's a shore.

Why was the blood cell brokenhearted? It loved in vein.

Why was the clock so nervous? It let itself get all wound up.

Which of Arthur's knights was most unnecessary? Sir Plus.

When is a whisper not a whisper? When it's aloud.

When is a shellfish not a shellfish? When it's a baloney.

What comes three times in every second and yet only once in a million years? E.

Why was the girl not afraid of the sharks? They were man-eating sharks.

When is a tux not a tux? When it's a peril or a tire.

Why was the jazz musician so sweet? He played in jam sessions.

Knock! Knock! Who's there? **Zippers.** Zippers who? **Zipper D. Doodah and Zipper D. Day.**

Why was George Washington buried at Mt. Vernon? Because he was dead.

Why'd Humpty Dumpty have his great fall? Because of a bad spring and summer salt.

Knock! Knock! Who's there? **Simon.** Simon who? **Simon the mood for love.**

Why'd Lancelot's horse trader scare away customers? He offered them knight mares.

Why'd the baker stop making doughnuts? He got bored of the hole thing.

Why'd the batter wear a rope to the plate? To tie up the score.

Why'd the cabbage leaf? Because it saw the banana split.

Why'd the cannibal eat his parents' sisters? He was an aunt-eater.

Why'd the cowboy look for the missing cattle in the forest? Because its leaves rustled.

Knock! Knock! Who's there? **Raoul.** Raoul who? **Raoul out the barrel.**

Why'd the dog chase the newspaper truck? He wanted to keep up with the Times.

What would you get if a piano fell on a child? A flat minor.

Why was the letter soggy? Postage dew.

Why was the Egyptologist so interested in sarcophagi? It's easy to get wrapped up in them.

Why was the bee hot? The B made the oil boil.

If your hair is falling out, what can you do to keep it in? Get a bag.

Why'd the fool dance with a jelly jar? It said twist to open.

Why'd the fool put a clock under his desk? He wanted to get paid for working over time.

Why'd the fool put an extra muffler on his car? To keep it warmer in the winter.

When is a funeral not a funeral? When it's awake.

Why is an A like a blossom? A bee (B) goes after both.

How many revolutionaries does it take to change a light bulb? None, they believe everything else has to change.

Why'd the fool wear loud socks? So his feet wouldn't fall asleep.

Why'd the farmer name his rooster Robinson? Because it crew so.

Why'd the fly fly? Because the spider spied 'er.

Why'd the football player marry the cheerleader? He believed she'd be true to the end.

Why'd the horses march in protest? For more horse power.

Why'd the invisible man go mad? Out of sight, out of mind.

Why'd the mother carry her baby? The baby couldn't carry her.

Knock! Knock! Who's there? **Sue.** Sue who? **Sue prize! It's me!**

Why's a bee like a fire? Both make oil boil.

Why's a bull in a china shop like a fire? The sooner the better put out.

Why's a comet like Lassie? Both're stars with tails.

Why's a cowboy like storm cloud? One hold reins and the other rains.

Knock! Knock! Who's there? **Shirley M.** Shirley M. who? **Shirley M. glad you answered.**

Why's an eye like Jesus being scourged? Both are under the lash.

Why's a grape have religious significance? It's connected to Divine.

Why's a horse's sore throat twice as bad as that of any other animal? If it had one it'd be a hoarse horse.

Why's a losing team like meringue? Both have been beaten.

What do you get if you cross a parrot and a shark? A bird that'll talk your ear off.

Why's a pencil like a riddle? Both're useless without a point.

Why's a piano never sad? When it works, it plays.

Why's a piano such a wonderful instrument? Many are upright and the rest grand.

What do you get if you cross a turkey with a centipede? Enough drumsticks.

Why's a quadruped always a poor dancer? It has two left feet.

What do you get if you cross a cat with a dinosaur? A very big litterbox.

Why's a shoemaker like a clergyman? One saves soles and the other souls.

Why's a storm cloud like a monarch? One rains and the other reigns.

Knock! Knock! Who's there? **Theophilus.** Theophilus who? **Theophilus person is the one who won't open the door for a friend.**

Why's a storyteller with shoes on so unusual? Because he has tales coming out of his mouth and tongues on his feet.

Why's a zeppelin like the moon? Both get lighter as they get fuller.

What's a one word anagram formed from "new" and "door"? "One word".

Knock! Knock! Who's there? **Wire.** Wire who? **Wire are you asking?**

What do you get when you cross a bull and a porcupine? A cross bull.

How do you make an egg roll? Set it down and push it.

How many cubic meters of dirt can you take from a hole 1.23 by 4.56 by 7.89? None, because it's empty.

How can you tell if you're cross-eyed? If you can see eye-to-eye with yourself.

How many peas on average are in a pint? One P.

Why don't snakes use silverware? They have forked tongues.

What two contradictory things did Noah do to build the ark? Chop up trees he'd chopped down.

What do you get if you cross poison ivy with a four-leaf clover? A rash of good luck.

How can you take some away and still leave the whole? Take 'some" from "wholesome".

Knock! Knock! Who's there? **Oscar and Greta.** Oscar and Greta who? **Oscar no questions and Greta no lies.**

If you gave 5% to five charities, what time would it be? 4:45 or a quarter to five.

How many computer programmers does it take to change a light bulb? None, that's a hardware problem.

How did the skeleton know it was raining? It felt it in its bones.

What did the police do to Mark who claimed to have witnessed a crime? Question Mark.

How much is 4Q plus 6Q? 10Q. **You're welcome.**

What's worse than a toothache? A threethache.

Which of Arthur's knights was most outlandish? Sir Real.

When was the blind carpenter healed? When he picked up his hammer and saw!

If the whole country bought pink automobiles, what would we have? A pink car nation.

If you dropped a tomato on your toe, would it hurt? It would, if it was still in the can.

How many strong men does it take to change a light bulb? Only one, because a light bulb is easier to change than a heavy bulb.

Why doesn't the invisible man have any children? He's not apparent.

Knock! Knock! Who's there? **Duane.** Duane who? **Duane the pool! I'm dwowning out here!**

What do you get if you cross a hyena and a parrot? An animal that laughs at its own jokes.

Knock! Knock! Who's there? **Abigail.** Abigail who? **Abigail's a-blowing in!**

What do you get if you cross an octopus and a cat? An animal with eight arms and nine lives.

Knock! Knock! Who's there? **Comma.** Comma who? **Comma little closer and you'll see.**

Why is it so hard to fool a snake? You can't pull its leg.

What's the day after tomorrow? Threemorrow.

Why did the seagull land on the fish? It was a perch.

Why was the duck sent to the principal? For making wise quacks.

Knock! Knock! Who's there? **Matt.** Matt who? **Your welcome Matt.**

If your child swallowed a knife and fork, what would you do? Feed him with a spoon.

What rock group includes four dead and one assassinated? Mt. Rushmore.

What do you get if you cross a cat and an elephant? A neighborhood without dogs.

Knock! Knock! Who's there? **Adolph.** Adolph who? **Adolph in's swimming by!**

What do you get if you cross a mink and an octopus? A coat of arms.

If vegetarians only eat vegetables, what do humanitarians eat? Humans?!

Knock! Knock! Who's there? **Anna.** Anna who? **Anna gonna tell you, unless you say please.**

Knock! Knock! Who's there? **Dolores.** Dolores who? **Dolores be an England.**

What's the difference between a pony and a giraffe? One's a little hoarse and the
    other's completely mute.

Knock! Knock! Whose there? **Mary.** Mary who? **Mary Christmas.**

What do you call a tobacco-chewing clone? A spitting image.

Knock! Knock! Who's there? **Yolanda.** Yolanda who? **Yolanda big fish when you use the
    right bait.**

What's worst than tendonitis? Elevendonitis.

Why don't chickens play baseball? Every pitch is a fowl ball.

What begins with T, ends with T and is full of T? Teapot.

What do English channel sea monsters eat? Fish and ships.

Which of Arthur's knights walked around the moat? Sir Cumference.

What would you call a campsite for 100 campers? Tenty.

What comes twice in a moment yet only once in a million years? M.

What's do you need to know to teach a lion tricks. More tricks than the lion.

Name a word that can be said faster by adding a syllable? Fast.

Knock! Knock! Who's there? **Shirley.** Shirley who? **Shirley you can open the door to find**

out.

Why did Hannibal the Cannibal lose his job? He tried to butter up his boss.

What's another name for semi-amnesia? Twogetfulness.

What would a duck wear to his wedding? A duxedo.

What would you call your parents' sister's older sister? Deodorant.

What's glacial in two letters? IC (icy).

Which of Arthur's knights had a carriage? Sir Rey.

Knock! Knock! Who's there? **Alison.** Alison who? **Alison to you if you'll listen to me.**

Watch do you call someone who oversees children at play? A game warden.

What has two eyes but can't see? A needle in a tornado.

What has fifty legs but can't walk? A half a centipede.

Why did you drop out of beauty school? Every test was a make-up test.

What do you get if you cross a parrot and a woodpecker? A telegrapher.

What geometric figure is like a lost parrot? Polygon.

How many grad students does it take to change a light bulb? Less than 1/100, because they have to change hundreds.

What happened to the cabbage and the tomato that raced? The cabbage was a head, but the was able to ketchup.

What's the occupational hazard of those who break wild horses? Broncitis.

How many lawyers does it take to change a light bulb? That depends on how many you can afford.

What was the historian's favorite quiz show? The Dating Game.

What's putrefaction in two letters? DK (decay).

What's the difference between a barefoot boy and an Arctic explorer? One wears no shoes, the other snowshoes.

How many quantum mechanics does it take to change a light bulb? None, because when they locate the bulb they can't turn it and when they turn it they can't locate it.

What's the difference between a cat and a comma? One has claws at the end of its paws, the other's a pause at the end of its clause.

What's the difference between a piano and a tuna? You can tune a piano, but you can can a tuna.

What do you get if you cross a rabbit and a skunk? Hare spray.

When is a hole not a hole? When is a knothole.

What's composition in two letters? SA (essay).

What do you get if you cross a wolf and rooster? An animal that crows at the sun and howls at the moon.

When is a jouster most likely to be unhorsed? At knightfall.

What's the difference between a boxer and cold victim? One knows his blows, the other blows his nose.

Where do animals go if they lose their tails? A re-tail store.

When is a building not a building? When it's aflame.

Which is the richest country in the world? Ireland, because its capital's always Dublin.

What do you get if you cross a starfish with a toad? Star warts.

What kind of water is healthiest? Well water.

What's effortless in two letters? EZ (easy).

Knock! Knock! Who's there? **Anita.** Anita who? **Open the door; Anita come in.**

How many schizophrenics does it take to change a light bulb? Only one but it seems like more.

Which word is most often spelled wrong? Wrong. **Right!**

How many liberals does it take to change a light bulb? One from every social, economic or ethnic group.

Why did the skeleton cross the road? It didn't have the guts.

What do you get if a piano falls on the army? A flat major.

Why didn't the boy help his sister? He couldn't be a brother and assist 'er too.

How many politicians does it take to change a light bulb? Two, one to change it and another one from the other party to change it back.

Your cat can operate the remote control?! Yes, it uses paws.

Knock! Knock! Who's there? **Rufus.** Rufus who? **Rufus on fire! Call the fire department!**

What's a conical tent in two letters? TP (teepee).

Knock! Knock! Who's there? **Ollie or Rex.** Ollie or Rex who? **Ollie or Rex shouldn't be in one basket.**

Why was the blood cell brokenhearted? It had loved in vein.

Why did the owl 'owl? Because the woodpecker would peck 'er.

How many mutants does it take to change a light bulb? 2/3.

What the difference between a baker and a buck? One kneads dough and the other needs a doe.

Why is the Greek immigrant like a French fry? One comes out of Greece and the other grease.

How many pollsters does it take to change a light bulb? One plus or minus one.

Why's a church bell like a banana? One gets pealed and the other peeled.

What's the difference between a carpenter and sixteen ounces? One weights a pound and the other pounds away.

Why do monks fry fish during Lent? They're not chicken fryers.

How many supreme court justices does it take to change a light bulb? 5/9

Why is the Congress like a head cold? Sometimes the ayes (eyes) have it and sometimes the no's (nose).

Knock! Knock! Who's there? **Ben.** Ben who? **Ben knocking so long my hand hurts.**

Why'd the tanner cross the tannery? To get to the other hide.

Knock! Knock! Who's there? **Juana.** Juana who? **Juana come out and play?**

How many senators does it take to change a light bulb? Two to sponsor the bill and thirty-one more to make a quorum.

Why did the traffic light turn red? It had to change in public.

Knock! Knock! Who's there? **Watson.** Watson who? **Watson TV tonight? Anything good?**

Why is a honeymoon suite like an empty room? Neither has a single person in it.

How many sociologists does it take to change a light bulb? None, they'd try to find out why the light bulb needs changing.

Knock! Knock! Who's there? **Sam 'n' Janet.** Sam and Janet who? Sam 'n' Janet Ev'ning...

Why is the good Samaritan like a horse? One stops for woe the other for whoa.

Knock! Knock! Who's there? **Will.** Will who? **Will you ever open the door to find out?**

What do you get if you cross an elephant and an insect? A forget-me-gnat.

How many manic-depressives does it take to change a light bulb? 1/2, because otherwise they'd change it back.

One. **How many psychics does it take to change a light bulb?**

What's the difference between a pet and a small-time painter? One shed its coat and the other coat a shed.

Why is a mouse like hay? The cat'll eat one and the cattle eat the other.

Which of Arthur's knights ate steak? Sir Loin.

How many surgeons does it take to change a light bulb? None, they'd wait for a donor light bulb and then just do a filament transplant.

Knock! Knock! Who's there? **Leena.** Leena who? **Leena little closer and I'll whisper it to you.**

Why is Saturday night so important to Julius' girlfriend? That's when Julius sees her.

Knock! Knock! Who's there? **Sadie.** Sadie who? **Sadie word please and I'll tell you.**

What did the shoemaker name his daughter? Peggy.

What do you get if you cross porcupine and a polecat? A very lonesome animal.

Why is your blouse with eight buttons the most attractive? With it you must fascinate.

Knock! Knock! Who's there? **Afghan.** Afghan who? **Afghan away because you wouldn't open the door.**

Why is Adam famous for being a runner? Because he was first in the Human race.

How many mathematicians does it take to change a light bulb? None, because the first light bulb has already been changed and the rest can be assumed changed by extrapolation.

Why is a teacher like an optometrist? They both test pupils.

What's worse than a bad forgery? A good fivegery.

What do you get if you cross a Pekingese with a Pomeranian? A Peeking Pom.

How many terrorists does it take to change a light bulb? None, because want to destroy the light bulb not change it.

Knock! Knock! Who's there? **Celeste.** Celeste who? **Celeste time I'm telling you. Open up!**

Why is a zeppelin like the moon? Both get lighter as they get fuller.

What did the dancer name her daughter? Grace.

Why you call your giant salamander Tiny? Because it's my newt.

What happens if a duck flies upside-down? It quacks up.

How many directors does it take to change a light bulb? Only one, but he changes it over and over and over again.

Knock! Knock! Who's there? **Colleen.** Colleen who? **Colleen up you room before you open this door. Did all the animals on Noah's ark come in pairs?** No the worms came in apples.

How do we know that Jesus raised cattle? Because he had many pair o' bulls.

What's worse than being forsaken and alone? Fivesaken and alone.

What did the gambler name his daughter? Bette.

Why are Sunday and Saturday the strongest days? The rest are week days.

Why did they call the baker mean? He beat the eggs and whipped the cream. **Knock! Knock!** Who's there? **Mary Lee.** Mary Lee who? **Mary Lee, Mary Lee, Mary Lee, Mary Lee, life is but a dream.**

How do you know if it's Enoch at the door? 'E knocks.

What time on the sixth day was Adam created? A little before Eve.

Who was known as a Mathematician in the Bible? Moses, he wrote the book of Numbers.

Knock! Knock! Who's there? **Olive.** Olive who? **Olive down the street, neighbor.**

Why was Abraham's niece turned into salt? Because she was dissatisfied with her lot.

What did Adam say on December 25th? It's Christmas, Eve!

Knock! Knock! Who's there? **Gen. Lee.** Gen. Lee who? **Gen. Lee I'd use the doorbell, but yours didn't work.**

What did the porter name his daughter? Carrie.

How'd Adam and Eve feel when they left the Garden of Eden? They were really put out.

Knock! Knock! Who's there? **Amanda Lynn.** Amanda Lynn who? **Amanda Lynn player.**

What happened in the first baseball game ever? In the big inning, Eve stole first, Adam stole second and Cain struck out Abel.

Where is the first tennis match mentioned in the Bible? When Joseph served in Pharaoh's court.

Why does it get hot in the stadium after the game? The fans are gone.

Why did the doctor make a house call? Its chimney had the flu.

Why could Jonah be eaten by the big fish? He was only a minor prophets!

Knock! Knock! Who's there? **Eve and Herman.** Eve and Herman who? **Eve and her man, Adam.**

Why didn't the Teddy bear eat dessert? It was stuffed.

How do we know Peter was a rich fisherman? By his net income.

What do you get if you saw a jokester in two? A half-wit.

Which of Arthur's knights was the most entertaining? Sir Cuss.

What did the chocolate bar say to the lollipop? Hello, sucker!

What gets dirtier as it gets whiter? A chalkboard.

What's the difference between a factory guard and a pickpocket? One watches steel and the other steals watches.

What comes once in a century but three times in four hundred years? R.

A hundred feet in the air, this still has its back on the ground. What is it? A flipped-over centipede.

Which New Testament book has a fruit in it? Phi-lemon.

How much is half of five? Four, when the other half is the E and F.

Knock! Knock! Who's there? **Amoeba.** Amoeba who? **Amoeba wrong, but I don't think you're opening the door yet.**

What's the first rule of kayaking? You can't have your kayak and heat it too.

How can you take one from six to get nine? Taking away S leaves IX.

Knock! Knock! Who's there? **Stan.** Stan who? **Stan back, cause I'm about to sneeze.**

What kind of stones can't be found in the ocean? Dry ones.

Which month has 28 days? All of them.

Which of Arthur's knights made pancakes? Sir Rupy.

Why did Hugh the Abbot stop flower sales? Only Hugh can prevent florist friars.

Where would you find rabbits in Paris? The hutch back of Notre Dame.

Why aren't there many penguins in Great Britain? They're afraid of Wales.

What did the beachcomber name the cat he found? Sandy Claws.

When does a B come after U? When you threaten the bee.

Knock! Knock! Who's there? **Mary and Abby.** Mary and Abby who? **Mary Christmas and Abby New Year.**

Why was the cafeteria clock always slow? Every meal it went back four seconds.

What do you get if you cross Sponge Bob with Einstein? Sponge Bob SmartyPants.

If a hydrant has H_2O on the inside, what does it have on the outside? K9P. (canine pee)

What would you find in the exact center of Paris? R.

How can you take four from seven and get five? Taking SEEN from SEVEN leaves V.

What's the difference between a jeweler and a jailer? One sells watches and the other watches cells.

What kind of bone gets shorter after it gets longer? A trombone.

Who saw Godzilla stomp on the restaurant? The diners saw the dinosaur.

What's the difference between a false friend and an undertaker? They're the first and the last to let you down.

Can you name five sets of twins from the Bible? Jacob and Esau, Perez and Zerah, the two Samuels, two Peters and two Timothies.

If Noah got milk from the cow and goat, what did he get from the ducks? Quackers.

What's the difference between an unemployed man and a feather bed? One is hard up and the other is soft down.

What kind of lights should Noah have had on the ark? Floodlights.

Why couldn't Noah go fishing? He only had two worms!

Knock! Knock! Who's there? **Noah.** Noah who? **Noah good book of riddles and rhymes?**

Why do sharks swim in salt water? Pepper water makes them sneeze.

Knock! Knock! Who's there? **Afghanistan.** Afghanistan who? **Afghanistan here all night until you open the door.**

If I have half a dozen apples and you take away two, how many do you have? Two.

Why do chickens lay eggs? If they dropped them, they'd break.

Knock! Knock! Who's there? **Jess.** Jess who? **Jess me and my shadow.**

What's Godzilla's favorite sport? Squash!

Why did the cookie go to the doctor? It was feeling crumby.

What does the sheik use to season his food? Sultan pepper.

Knock! Knock! Who's there? **Megan, Elise and Chuck.** Megan, Elise and Chuck who? **Megan, Elise and Chuck Kennit twice, seeing who's been naughty and nice.**

Where was Solomon's temple located? The same as ours, on the side of his head.

What goes up a chimney down, but can't go down a chimney up? An umbrella.

What 11-letter word does almost everyone pronounce incorrectly? Incorrectly.

Knock! Knock! **Who's there?** Eiffel. Eiffel who? **Eiffel down and hurt myself.**

Would you rather have a tiger eat you or a lion? I'd rather the tiger eat the lion!

What kind cheese is made backwards? Edam.

Which takes longer – running from first base to second or from second to third?
   Second to third, because there's a short stop in between.

Why was the fool staring at his juice? The container said "Concentrate".

Why was the stool afraid of the chair? The chair was armed.

What's the most difficult bow to tie? A Rainbow.

Knock! Knock! Who's there? **Allison.** Allison who? **Allison Wonderland.**

Which of Arthur's knights scouted out the enemy? Sir Veyor.

What has even more lives than a cat? A frog that croaks every night.

What's the difference between a shipwrecked sailor and a blindfolded man? One can't
   go to see and the other can't see to go.

How can you take four from eight and get one?, Taking GETH from eight leaves I.

Which of Arthur's knights was the most useful? Sir Vant.

What do penguins sing on birthdays? "Freeze a Jolly Good Fellow".

What's the difference between a habitual sinner and a soap that floats? One sins
   without thinking and the other thins without sinking.

Knock! Knock! Who's there? **Amos.** Amos who? **Amos Quito bit me.**

Knock! Knock! Who's there? **Arthur.** Arthur who? **Arthur any more at home like you?**

When did Eve eat the forbidden fruit? Early in the Fall.

Which New Testament book has an insect in it? Ti-moth-y.

Knock! Knock! Who's there? **Celeste.** Celeste who? **Celeste time I'm going to answer you.**

Why did the atheist kittens become Christian? They finally opened their eyes.

Knock! Knock! Who's there? **Butcher.** Butcher who? **Butcher arms around me.**

Knock! Knock! Who's there? **Minerva.** Minerva who? **Minerva's wreck from knock-knocking.**

What chips and peels but isn't paint? A potato.

What vegetable didn't Noah take on the ark? Leeks.

What do you call a litter of ten kittens? Catty.

How can you take two from six and get ten? Taking S and I from six leaves X.

How many evolutionists does it take to change a light bulb? One but it takes 100,000 years.

What do you get if you add eight teacups and four teacups? Ten dozen.

Knock! Knock! Who's there? **Wendy.** Wendy who? **Wendy moon comes over the mountain.**

How can you avoid getting wrinkles? Don't sleep in your clothes.

How can you buy four suits for a dollar? Buy a deck of cards.

What do you call a penguin in the desert? Lost.

Why did the turtle cross the road? To get to the Shell station.

Knock! Knock! Who's there? **Max.** Max who? **Max no difference. You ought to open the door.**

What's a mummy's favorite music? Wrap.

What's the difference between ammonia and pneumonia? One is found in bottles, the other chests.

How do you get fur from a bear? By the fastest transportation you can.

Knock! Knock! Who's there? **Hugh.** Hugh who? **Yoo-hoo to you too.**

How many apples on an average grow on an apple tree? All of them.

How do you make an elephant float? Put an elephant and a scoop of ice cream into a glass of soda.

Why was Abraham considered smart? He knew a Lot.

Knock! Knock! Who's there? **Michael Roe.** Michael Roe who? **Michael Roe'd the boat ashore.** Alleluia!

What's the difference between a coyote and a flea? One howls on the prairie and the other prowls on the hairy.

When was pork first eaten? In the Sauce Age.

What do Aussies call a cat that's swallowed a duck? A duck-filled fatty puss.

How does a Hawaiian baritone laugh? With a low ha.

Knock! Knock! Who's there? **Lettuce.** Lettuce who? **Lettuce it and you'll see.**

How does a king open the castle gate? With his monarch key.

Knock! Knock! Who's there? **Chester.** Chester who? **Chester minute and I'll see.**

Why did the bubble gum cross the road? It was stuck to the chicken's foot.

What do you call a group of ten crying girls? Missty.

Knock! Knock! Who's there? **Irving.** Irving who? **Irving a good time, wish you were here.**

How many bricks does it take to finish a house? Just the last one.

Why do elephants travel in herds? Because if they traveled in flocks they'd confuse the sheepdogs.

What did the buffalo parents say when their son left the herd? Bye, son.

Knock! Knock! Who's there? **Alex.** Alex who? **Alex you again, "Please, let me in."**

How would you find Lancelot in the dark? With a knight light.

How much pet food should you get for a dollar? None, it doesn't eat.

What did the vet say when he found the bull had eaten dynamite? A-bomb-in-a-bull!

How many psychologists does it take to change a light bulb? One, but the light bulb really has to want to change.

How do you improve education by buying lottery tickets? Ever time you lose, you get a little smarter.

Knock! Knock! Who's there? **Dexter.** Dexter who? **Dexter halls with boughs of holly. Fa, la, la, la, la, la, la, la, la!**

Who in the Bible spoke as a baby? Job cursed the day he was born.

Knock! Knock! Who's there? **Luke.** Luke who? **Luke and see.**

If 9 comes after 8, and 10 comes after 9, what comes after 10? Jack.

If an athlete can get athlete's foot, what might an astronaut get? Missile-toe.

What do you get when you cross a midget and an electrician? A short circuit.

How many Democrats does it take to change a light bulb? Four, one to do it and three to share the experience.

Knock! Knock! Who's there? **Caesar**. Caesar who? **Caesar jolly good fellow.**

What would you call a hump-less camel? Humphrey.

What's better than wonderful? Twoderful.

If you divided your profits equally between yourself and three partners, what time would it be? 3:45 (a quarter to four)

What's the name of the compulsive talkers self-help group? On-and-on Anon.

What's worse than being stubborn and asinine? Stubborn and asiten.

Knock! Knock! Who's there? **Nobel**. Nobel who? **Nobel, so I'm knocking.**

What do you get if you add four teaspoons to six teaspoons? A hundred spoons.

Which of Arthur's knights drank "for medicinal purposes"? Sir Rum.

What gets whiter the dirtier it gets? A chalkboard.

Why was the painter unproductive? When he tried, he just drew a blank.

Knock! Knock! Who's there? **Thor**. Thor who? **Thorry, I mutht have the wrong addreth.**

What do you call a dinosaur that never gives up? A try-try-trycertops.

Did you hear about the accident at the cannery? A worker got canned!

Did you apply for the job at the coffeemaker factory? Yeah, it doesn't pay much, but has lots of perks.

How can you protect yourself from wild African dogs? Light jackal lanterns.

What insect is best at math? A rithme tick.

What happens to a shellfish that over-exercises? It becomes mussel-bound.

What do you get when you cross a small dog with an urban dove? A terrier pigeon. **What would you call a prophetic cobbler?** A psychic heeler.

How much money did Noah have? $7.02, four bills from the ducks and platypuses, two greenbacks from the frogs, one buck and two cents from the skunks.

What do you call an unemployed jester? Nobody's fool.

Why didn't the walkingstick walk across the road? It was a walkingstick-in-the-mud.

What reptile lurks in the dark between buildings? An alley gator.

Why don't crocodiles use microwaves? They prefer croc pots.

What do you call someone who commits fraud via telephone? A telephony.

Why did the bear go into the woods to hibernate? For rest.

Why did the worm cross the road? The early bird was after it.

Why didn't the early bird cross the road? It was a chicken.

What did the ceiling say to the walls? Meet me at the corner.

Why can't I have your cheese? 'Cause it's nacho cheese; it's my cheese!

How does the gingerbread man make his bed? With a cookie sheet.

What's the difference between a policeman and a police dog? One has a whole uniform and the other only pants.

Knock! Knock! Who's there? **Deluxe.** Deluxe who? **Deluxe Smith, here to fix de lux.**

Why do flamingos stand on one leg? If they lifted their other one they'd fall down.

Knock! Knock! Who's there? **Max.** Max who? **Max no difference; just open the door.**

What would happen if no doe fawns were born? Stag nation.

When is a woman not a woman? When she's abroad.

What's the difference between a rabid rabbit and counterfeit money? One's a mad bunny and the other bad money.

Why did the T. rex cross they road? Who'd want to try and stop it!

When is an anchor not an anchor? When it's a whey.

What would you call a zebra-striped octopus with whip-like tentacles? Whackin' blight.

What do you call an alligator adapted to cold? A refriger gator.

You have a cow trim you grass? Yes, a lawn mooer.

Why do hummingbirds hum? They can't remember the lyrics.

What happened to the ice that couldn't make it as a cube? It was crushed.

When is a plane not a plane? When it's a loft.

Why is a mechanical bull like a silver dollar? They're metallic from head to tail.

What's thrown out when needed, but taken in when not? An anchor.

Why didn't the turkey cross the road? It was Thanksgiving.

What would you call a marsupial that explodes? A bombwat.

Why couldn't the astronaut go to the moon? It was full.

What did the lamb say to its mother after suckling? Thank ewe mother.

What's the difference between a butcher and an insomniac? One weighs a steak and the other stays awake.

What do you get if you cross a mustang and a dinosaur? A broncosaurus.

What's the difference between a rain gutter and a sun-blind outfielder? One catches drops and the other drops catches.

Why do elephants have trunks? Because they don't have luggage racks.

Knock! Knock! Who's there? **Police!** Police who? **Police open the door.**

What's the most popular dog breed? The trend setter.

Why did the human cannonball quit? He was too high caliber and couldn't be fired.

What's the difference between a liar and a sold-out bakery? One has a pack of lies and the other a lack of pies.

What was the decision when the pig swallowed the baseball? An inside the pork home run.

What's the difference between a shipment of fruit and a cookie-less serving dish? One is a crate of plums and the other a plate of crumbs.

What's the difference between a cooking student who passes and one who doesn't? One learned a bunch, the other burned a lunch.

What do you get if you cross a pig and a dinosaur? Jurassic pork.

Why don't grizzlies wear hats? Because they're bear-headed.

Why was the gnu moaning? It had gnumonia.

Did they catch the trespassing paparazzi? Yes, he left his prints at the scene of the crime.

Why'd the fool put a Barby doll on his grill? He wanted to have a Barbieque.

If Mary's little lamb followed her to school, where'd her little cow go? The school calfeteria.

Did they find the pig thieves? Yes, someone squealed.

Which primate can fly? The hot-air baboon.

What's harder than quitting cold turkey? Trying to tapir off.

Knock! Knock! Who's there? **Izzy.** Izzy who? **Izzy home? I wanna see'im.**

How did the gnu cross the river? In a cagnu.

What do you get if you cross a baboon and a parrot? A blabboon.

When is a zeppelin not a zeppelin? When it's a float.

Why didn't the mutants marry? They couldn't see eye to eye to eye.

What was the name of the matador who got injured? Gord.

What do you call a sun-loving Mediterranean manatee? A tan-a-mee.

Why aren't elephants allowed in the pool? They can't keep their trunks up.

Knock! Knock! Who's there? **Andrew.** Andrew who? **Ann drew a picture of you; open the door and I'll show you.**

Your gardener quit? Yes, he threw in the trowel.

How many sheep does it take to make a sweater? Sheep don't make sweaters! Sheep make wool.

What noise could wake up everyone in the whole world? Noah's rooster.

What do you get if you cross a catfish and a piranha? A purrahna.

What is in Matthew and John, but not in Luke or Mark? H.

What's the difference between a blacksmith and an identity thief? One checks his forge and the other forges checks.

Why was the football team acquitted? They had a strong defense.

What do you call an ear-less bear? A bee (B).

Why can't you fool a snake? It has no leg to pull.

What has five hundred legs but can't walk. A half a millipede.

What happened when the frog's lily-pad broke down? It got toad away.

What do you get when you cross frog and a rabbit? A bunny ribbit.

What's the difference between a dog and a dogwood? One grows bark and the other makes itself bark.

Can you get fur from a werewolf? As fur as I can get!

What kind of killer bees don't die? Zomb-bees.

What do you get if you cross a kangaroo and a snake? A jump rope.

Why don't polar bears marry? They get cold feet.

Why is G like midnight? Both at in the middle of night.

What do you get if you cross a sheep and a baboon? A baaboon.

What do you call a cat that teaches cheetahs to cheat? A teechah.

What would you call a tiny vole predator? A vole weebil.

Why do little piglets eat so much? To become big pigs.

What did the farmer name his hatchling? Chick Ken.

Did they catch the vegetable thieves? Yes, one of them spilled the beans.

What's a doctor's favorite meat? Cured ham.

Why did the fool dance with his ketchup bottle? It said twist to open.

What did the baker go to the dentist? His pie crust needed a filling.

Did they catch the anchor thieves? No, they got aweigh.

Why are giraffes so stubborn? It takes them a long time to swallow their pride.

Why was the five-legged mutant happy with his tailor? His pants fit like a glove.

Where do boats go when they get seasick? The dock.

Why are walruses so wrinkly? They never iron.

What can you do with a smashed tomato? Make some tomato paste.

How was the sale at the sporting goods store? It was an oar deal.

How was the sale at the furniture store? I'm re-covering.

Why did the math book go to the doctor? It had many internal problems.

Why don't shrimp share? They're shellfish.

How do you get good at woodcarving? Whittle by whittle.

Why did the frog go to the doctor? It felt like it was going to croak.

Why can you play hide and seek in the mountains? They peak.

Why are atoms hard to understand? The make up almost everything.

What is a ship captain's least favorite vegetable? Leeks.

Why did the children cross the playground? To get to the other slide.

Why did the sitter call the police? The baby was resisting a rest.

Why can't leopards play hide and seek? They're always spotted.

When is it time for a teacher to take vacation? When she has no class left.

When does the chicken ever come before the egg? In the dictionary.

Why wasn't Lincoln impeached? He was in a cent.

Why did the freight elevator go to the doctor? It was coming down with something.

Where does Santa vote? At the North poll.

What did the burglers steal from the music store? They made off with the lute.

What did the calendar thief get? Twelve months.

What did the glove say to the ball? Catch you later.

What do you call road kill that doesn't smell any more? Ex-stink.

Where does the king keep his army? In his sleevey.

What do you call the Unsinkable Man? Bob.

What grows up and down at the same time? A gosling.

Why was the little ant confused? All its uncles were ants.

What did the digital clock say to the grandfather clock? Look, gramps, no hands!

What do you call colliding tyrannosaurs? T. wrecks.

What do you call a toothless grizzly? A gummy bear.

What do you call it when you're not O blood type. A Type O typo.

Why was the Energizer Bunny arrested? For battery.

What do you get when you cross a parrot and a dinosaur? A thesaurus.

What do you get when you cross a duck and a rooster? Awakened at the quack of dawn.

Which puns are the worst? Ones about German sausage.

Knock! Knock! Who's there? **Boo.** Boo who? **Why are you crying?** This is the last riddle!

THE ANIMAL FAIR

I went to the animal fair. The birds and the beasts were there.
The big baboon by the light of the moon was combing his auburn hair.
You ought to have seen the monk. He climbed up the elephant's trunk.
The elephant sneezed and fell on his knees,
But what became of the monk? The monk? The monk?

The monk flew up into the air and landed in the cage with the bear.
The big black bear with the grizzly hair gave him a frightening stare,
So the monkey climbed up the bars, heading for the parked cars,
But he only found himself on the ground suddenly looking at stars.

He went to the animal doc, who was extracting a tooth from a croc,
But he quickly time found when he heard a sound that made the whole fair rock.
The elephant had sneezed again, this time falling on his rear end,
So the monk then ran to the bandstand trying to find him a friend.

From tuba to fiddle he flew, from drum to bassoon to kazoo.
He finally stopped when a balloon popped near the old kangaroo.
By then he was frazzled indeed. He another shock didn't need,
But wouldn't you know then had to show the keepers with animal feed.

The lions and tigers roared. The giraffes silently implored.
Each and every beast craved its personal feast, while the ape escape explored.
Finally he leapt the fence and never has been seen hence,
So no one can say to this very day what became of the monk, the monk, the monk.

THE ANTS GO MARCHING

The ants go marching one by one. Hurrah! Hurrah!
The ants go marching one by one. Hurrah! Hurrah!
The ants go marching one by one.
The little one stops to suck his thumb
And they all go marching in the big parade.

The ants go marching two by two. Hurrah! Hurrah!
The ants go marching two by two. Hurrah! Hurrah!
The ants go marching two by two. The little one stops to tie his shoe.
And they all go marching in the big parade.

The ants go marching three by three. Hurrah! Hurrah!

The ants go marching three by three. Hurrah! Hurrah!
The ants go marching three by three. The little one stops to climb a tree.
And they all go marching in the big parade.

The ants go marching four by four. Hurrah! Hurrah!
The ants go marching four by four. Hurrah! Hurrah!
The ants go marching four by four.
The little one stops to sleep some more.
And they all go marching in the big parade.

The ants go marching five by five. Hurrah! Hurrah!
The ants go marching five by five. Hurrah! Hurrah!
The ants go marching five by five. The little one stops to joke and jive.
And they all go marching in the big parade.

The ants go marching six by six. Hurrah! Hurrah!
The ants go marching six by six. Hurrah! Hurrah!
The ants go marching six by six. The little one stops to do some tricks.
And they all go marching in the big parade.

The ants go marching seven by seven. Hurrah! Hurrah!
The ants go marching seven by seven. Hurrah! Hurrah!
The ants go marching seven by seven. The little one stops to pay to heaven.
And they all go marching in the big parade.

The ants go marching eight by eight. Hurrah! Hurrah!
The ants go marching eight by eight. Hurrah! Hurrah!
The ants go marching eight by eight. The little one stops to shut the gate.
And they all go marching in the big parade.

The ants go marching nine by nine. Hurrah! Hurrah!
The ants go marching nine by nine. Hurrah! Hurrah!
The ants go marching nine by nine. The little one stops to read a sign.
And they all go marching in the big parade.

The ants go marching ten by ten. Hurrah! Hurrah!
The ants go marching ten by ten. Hurrah! Hurrah!
The ants go marching ten by ten. The little one stops to say "The end!"
And they all stop marching in the big parade.

AIN'T WE CRAZY

The sky was dark and gloomy while the sun was shining bright.
The lightning and the thunder danced around with all their might.
The moon cast forth a shadow, though the air was black as night
And everything that you could see was hidden out of sight.

The crickets played their mouth harps, while a frog played on its drum
And the dogs barked to the music, while the hummingbirds did hum.
Horseflies galloped to the beat and mayflies did their dance
And insects of all kinds lined up to wait for their next chance.

It was evening and the sunrise was just setting in the west,
When the little fishes in the treetops were all cuddled in their nest,
As the wind was blowing bubbles, lightning shot from left to right,
Then it shot from top to bottom, illuminating the whole night.

The cows were making cowlicks. The bells were ringing wet.
The bumblebees were bumbling with a towelette.
A man stepped into a stable and came out a little hoarse,
So he jumped upon his golf cart and rowed around the course.

It was midnight on the ocean, not a streetcar was in sight,
As he stepped into a cybercafe to get himself a byte.
The young man behind the counter was a woman old and gray,
Who used to peddle shoestrings on the road to Mandalay.

"Good evening, sir!" the woman said. Her eyes were bright with tears,
As she put her head between her feet and stood that way for years.
Her children all were orphans except one tiny tot,
Who lived in the house across the street upon a vacant lot.

As he gazed through the oaken door a whale went drifting by.
Its six legs hanging in the air, so he kissed that girl goodbye."
This story has a moral as you can plainly see:
"Don't mix your gin with whiskey on the deep and dark blue sea."

AWAY UP NORTH

Away up north where the aurora's at, a grasshopper hopped onto a gnat.
Both insects cried out in great surprise:

"Away out west where shore meets sea, a grasshopper hopped on a redwood tree.
The redwood cried out, 'I would advise,
Away back east where Liberty stands, A grasshopper hopped into her hands.
The statue said, "I can't compromise.

Away down south where cotton grows,
A grasshopper hopped between the rows, And between hops the hopper cries:
'Away up high in insectoid space,
The Grasshoppers the Gnats replace, the galaxy to colonize.'"'"

BABY BUMBLEBEE

O, I'm bringing home a baby bumblebee. Won't my mommy be so proud of me?
'Cause I'm bringing home a baby bumblebee. Buzzy, buzzy, buzzy – ooh it stung me!

O, I'm bringing home a baby rattlesnake. Won't my mommy shiver and shake?
'Cause I'm bringing home a baby rattlesnake. Rattle, rattle, rattle – ooh it bit me!

O, I'm bringing home a baby turtle. Won't my mommy really pop her girdle?
'Cause I'm bringing home a baby turtle. Snappy, snappy, snappy – ooh it bit me!

O, I'm bringing home a baby dinosaur.
Won't my mommy fall right through the floor?
'Cause I'm bringing home a baby dinosaur. Gobble, gobble, gobble – ooh it ate ...

A BAREFOOT BOY WITH SHOES ON

Oh, a barefoot boy with shoes on came walking down the street.
His hands were full of pockets and his shoes were full of feet.
He was an only child, you know, his mother's pride and joy,
His only sister was a girl and his brother was a boy.

His brother was a triple, his sister was a twin,
His legs were fastened to his knees just below the chin
And both his feet joined his ankles several inches from his shoulder.
He grew up to be a young man who every day grew older.

He was married to a woman who soon became his wife.
She weighed four hundred sixty and was skinny all her life.
Her head was filled with notions and her mouth was full of tongue.
They had a dozen children all born when they were young.

Six boys and five girls and then another child,

They always tried to raise them right, not too mild or too wild,
And late in the evening they'd send them off to bed,
Not sure if they were sleeping, but knowing they'd all been fed.

The youngest was the baby, but the oldest was one first.
The good ones were the best, but the bad one was the worst.
They never knew their father's age, but they always had a hunch
That he was born before their time and the oldest of the bunch.

They became gents and ladies, I knew them all quite well.
The girls all went to Heaven and the boys all went out West.

THE BEAR WENT OVER THE MOUNTAIN

The bear went over the mountain. The bear went over the mountain.
The bear went over the mountain to see what he could see,
To see what he could see, to see what he could see.
The bear went over the mountain to see what he could see.

The other side of the mountain, the other side of the mountain,
The other side of the mountain, that's what he could see.
Oh, that's what he could see. That's what he could see.
The other side of the mountain, That's what he could see.

He saw another mountain. He saw another mountain.
He saw another mountain across the clear blue sea,
Across the clear blue sea, across the clear blue sea.
He saw another mountain across the clear blue sea.

The bear had lunch on the mountain. The bear had lunch on the mountain.
The bear had lunch on the mountain and drank a cup of tea,
And drank a cup of tea. and drank a cup of tea.
The bear had lunch on the mountain and then he went to sleep!

BILLY BOY

Where have you been all the day, Billy Boy, Billy Boy?
Where have you been all the day, charming Billy?
I have been to seek a wife. She's the joy of my life.
She's a young thing and cannot leave her mother.

Did she ask you to come in, Billy Boy, Billy Boy?
Did she ask you to come in, charming Billy?

She did ask me to come in. She's a dimple on her chin.
She's a young thing and cannot leave her mother.

Can she bake a cherry pie, Billy Boy, Billy Boy?
Can she bake a cherry pie, charming Billy?
She can bake a cherry pie quick as a cat can wink its eye.
She's a young thing and cannot leave her mother.

Does she often go to church, Billy Boy, Billy Boy?
Does she often go to church, charming Billy?
Yes, she often goes to church in a bonnet white as birch.
She's a young thing and cannot leave her mother.

Is she fit to be a wife, Billy Boy, Billy Boy?.
Is she fit to be a wife, charming Billy?
She's as fit to be a wife as a fork fits to a knife.
She's a young thing and cannot leave her mother.

How old is she, Billy Boy, Billy Boy?
How old is she, charming Billy?
She's three times eight plus seven, twice ten and eleven.
She's a young thing and cannot leave her mother.

BINGO
There was a farmer had a dog and Bingo was his name-o.
B-I-N-G-O, B-I-N-G-O, B-I-N-G-O and Bingo was his name-o.
There was a farmer had a dog and Bingo was his name-o.
[clap]-I-N-G-O, [clap]-I-N-G-O, [clap]-I-N-G-O and Bingo was his name-o.

There was a farmer had a dog and Bingo was his name-o.
[two claps]-N-G-O, [two claps]-N-G-O, [two claps]-N-G-O and Bingo was his name-o.
There was a farmer had a dog and Bingo was his name-o.
[three claps]-G-O, [three claps]-G-O, [three claps]-G-O and Bingo was his name-o.

There was a farmer had a dog and Bingo was his name-o.
[four claps]-O, [four claps]-O, [four claps]-O, and Bingo was his name-o.
There was a farmer had a dog and Bingo was his name-o.
[five claps], [five claps], [five claps], and Bingo was his name-o.

THE BLUE-TAIL FLY

When I was young, I used to wait upon old master and pass his plate
And fetch the bottle when he got dry and brush away the blue-tail fly.
Jimmy crack corn and I don't care. Jimmy crack corn and I don't care,
Jimmy crack corn and I don't care. My master's gone away.

And when he'd ride in the afternoon, I'd follow with a hickory broom.
The pony being very shy, got bitten by the blue-tail fly.
Jimmy crack corn and I don't care. Jimmy crack corn and I don't care,
Jimmy crack corn and I don't care. My master's gone away.

One day he rode around the farm. The flies so numerous, they did swarm,
One chanced to bite him on the thigh. The devil take the blue-tail fly!
Jimmy crack corn and I don't care. Jimmy crack corn and I don't care,
Jimmy crack corn and I don't care. My master's gone away.

The pony run; he run; he pitch. He threw old master in a ditch.
He died and the jury wondered why. The verdict was: the blue-tailed fly.
Jimmy crack corn and I don't care. Jimmy crack corn and I don't care,
Jimmy crack corn and I don't care. My master's gone away.

They laid him under a 'simmon tree. His epitaph is there to see:
"Beneath the earth I'm forced to lie, a victim of the blue-tail fly".

CAMPTOWN RACES

Camptown ladies sing their song: "Doodah! Doodah!"
The Camptown racetrack's five miles long. O Doodah Day!
I come down there with my hat caved in. Doodah! Doodah!
I go back with a pocketful of tin. O Doodah Day!

Going to run all night. Going to run all day.
I'll bet my money on the bobtail nag.
Somebody bet on the bay.

The long-tail filly and the big black horse. Doodah! Doodah!
They fly the track and the both cut across. O Doodah Day!
The blind horse sticking in a big mud hole – Dooddah! Doodah! –
Can't touch bottom with a ten-foot pole. O Doodah Day!

Going to run all night. Going to run all day.

I'll bet my money on the bobtail nag. Somebody bet on the bay.

CAN'T GET TO HEAVEN
Oh, you can't get to Heaven on a trolley car, 'Cause a trolley car won't go that far.
Oh, you can't get to Heaven on a trolley car, But you can get to heaven with Jesus!
Oh, you can't get to Heaven in a ping pong ball 'Cause a ping pong ball is much too small.
Oh, you can't get to Heaven in a ping pong ball, But you can get to heaven with Jesus!

Oh, you can't get to Heaven in a rocking chair, 'Cause a rockin' chair don't go nowhere.
Oh, you can't get to Heaven in a rocking chair, But you can get to heaven with Jesus!
Oh, you can't get to Heaven on a rocket ship, 'Cause a rocket ship can't make the trip.
Oh, you can't get to Heaven on a rocket ship, But you can get to heaven with Jesus!

Oh, you can't get to heaven in a limousine, 'Cause there ain't that much gasoline.
Oh, you can't get to heaven in a limousine, But you can get to heaven with Jesus!
Oh, you can't get to Heaven with a pot of gold, 'Cause nothin' there is bought or sold.
Oh, you can't get to Heaven with a pot of gold, But you can get to heaven with Jesus!

Oh, you can't get to Heaven on a kangaroo, 'Cause a kangaroo just won't do!
Oh, you can't get to Heaven on a kangaroo, But you can get to heaven with Jesus!
Oh, you can't get to Heaven on a quarterhorse, 'Cause a quarterhorse is on the race course,
Oh, you can't get to Heaven on a quarter horse, But you can get to heaven with Jesus!

Oh, you can't get to Heaven in an SUV, 'Cause an SUV's not heavenly.
Oh, you can't get to Heaven in an SUV, But you can get to heaven with Jesus!
Oh, you can't get to Heaven on a pair of skis, Not even if you say "Pretty please!"
Oh, you can't get to Heaven on a pair of skis, But you can get to heaven with Jesus!

Oh, you can't get to Heaven on a pogo stick, 'Cause a pogo stick's not angelic.
Oh, you can't get to Heaven on a pogo stick, But you can get to heaven with Jesus!
Oh, you can't get to Heaven on roller skates; That's not the way to the pearly gates.
Oh, you can't get to Heaven on roller skates, But you can get to heaven with Jesus!

Oh, you can't get to Heaven on a jumbo jet, At least one ain't got there yet.
Oh, you can't get to Heaven on a jumbo jet, But you can get to heaven with Jesus!
Oh, you can't get to Heaven in a biscuit tin, 'Cause a biscuit tin's got biscuits in.
Oh, you can't get to Heaven in a biscuit tin, But you can get to heaven with Jesus!

Oh, you can't get to Heaven in an apple tree, 'Cause an apple tree's got roots you see.
Oh, you can't get to Heaven in an apple tree, But you can get to heaven with Jesus!

Oh, you can't get to Heaven in a leaky boat, 'Cause a leaky boat won't even float.
Oh, you can't get to Heaven in a leaky boat, But you can get to heaven with Jesus!

Oh there's one more thing I forgot to tell,
You can't get to heaven, if you go to that other place,
But you can get to heaven with Jesus!

THE CAT CAME BACK
Old Mr. Johnson had troubles of his own. The worse was a cat which wouldn't leave its home;
He tried and he tried to give the cat away, He gave it to a man going far, far away ...

But the cat came back the very next day, The cat came back,
He thought it was a goner, But the cat came back.
It would not stay away. It was back on his porch the very next day.

Johnson tried everything he knew to get the cat to stay away,
even took it up to Canada and told it there to stay ...

Away across the ocean he sent the cat at last. The ship only a day out taking water fast,
People all began to pray. The ship it was tossed.
Everyone was saved, but the ship's cat was lost...

THE CHIVALROUS SHARK
The most chivalrous fish of the ocean to ladies forbearing and mild,
Though his record be dark, is the man-eating shark, who will eat neither woman nor child.
He dines upon seamen and skippers, and tourists his hunger assuage,
And a fresh cabin boy will inspire him with joy, if he's past childhood age.
A doctor, a lawyer, a preacher, he'll gobble one any fine day,
But the ladies, God bless 'em, he'll only address 'em politely and go on his way.

I can readily cite you an instance where a lovely young lady of Breem,
Who was tender and sweet and delicious to eat fell into the bay with a scream.
She struggled and flounced in the water, and signaled in vain for her bar,
And she'd surely been drowned if she hadn't been found By a chivalrous man-eating shark.
He bowed in a manner most polished, thus soothing her impulses wild.
'Don't be frightened," he said, "I've been properly bred, and'll never eat woman nor child."

Then he proffered his fin and she took it -- such gallantry none can dispute --
While the passengers cheered as the vessel they neared and it fired a broadside in salute.
And they soon stood alongside the vessel, when a life-saving dinghy was lowered

With the pick of the crew, and her relatives too And the mate and the skipper aboard.

So they took her aboard in a jiffy, and the shark stood attention the while,
Then he raised on his flipper and ate up the skipper And went on his way with a smile.
And this shows that the prince of the ocean, to ladies forbearing and mild,
Though his record be dark is the man-eating shark, Who will eat neither woman nor child.

CLEMENTINE
In a cavern, in a cavern, excavating for a mine,
Lived a miner, forty-niner and his daughter Clementine.

O my darling, O my darling, O my darling Clementine.
You are lost and gone forever. Dreadful sorry, Clementine!

Light she was and like a fairy and her shoes were made of pine,
Herring boxes without topses, sandals were for Clementine.

Drove her ducklings to the water every morning just at nine.
Hit her foot against a splinter, fell into the foaming brine.

Ruby lips above the water, blowing bubbles soft and fine,
But, alas, I was no swimmer, so I lost my Clementine.

Then the miner, forty-niner, soon began to peak and pine,
Thought he oughter join his daughter. Now he's with his Clementine.

There's a churchyard on the hillside, where the flowers grow and twine.
There grow roses ;mongst the posies, fertilized by Clementine.

In my dreams she used to haunt me, robed in garlands soaked in brine,
Though in life I used to hug her, now she's dead, I draw the line.

Now you scouts may learn the moral of this little tale of mine,
Artificial respiration might have saved my Clementine.

How I missed her! How I missed her! How I missed my Clementine,
'Til I kissed her little sister and forgot 'bout Clementine.

COCKLES AND MUSSELS
In Dublin's fair city, where the girls are so pretty,

I first set my eyes on sweet Molly Malone,
As she wheeled her wheelbarrow through streets broad and narrow,
Crying "Cockles and mussels, alive, alive-o! Alive, alive-o! Alive, alive-o!",
Crying "Cockles and mussels, alive, alive-o!"

She was a fishmonger, but sure 'twas no wonder, For so were her father and mother before
And they each wheeled a wheelbarrow through streets broad and narrow,
Crying "Cockles and mussels, alive, alive-o! Alive, alive-o! Alive, alive-o!",
Crying "Cockles and mussels, alive, alive-o!"

She died of a fever and no one could save her And that was the end of sweet Molly Malone.
Her ghost wheels her wheelbarrow through streets broad and narrow,
Crying "Cockles and mussels, alive, alive-o! Alive, alive-o! Alive, alive-o!",
Crying "Cockles and mussels, alive, alive-o!"

THE DERBYSHIRE RAM

As I went down to Derby, sir, all on a market day,
I saw the biggest ram, sir, that ever was fed on hay.
All on a market day, sir, all on a market day,
I saw the biggest ram, sir, that ever was fed on hay.

He had so large a hoof, sir, a hoof so large and round
That when he put it down, sir, It covered an acre of ground.
This ram had four legs to walk on, sir. It had four legs to stand
And every leg he had, sir, stood on an acre of land.

The wool upon his back, sir, reached up into the sky.
The eagles built their nests there; I heard the young ones cry.
This ram jumped over a wall, sir, his tail caught on a briar,
It reached from Derby town, sir, to Leicestershire.

The men that fed this ram, sir, would feed him twice a day
And whenever his mouth opened, sir, he swallowed a rick of hay.
This ram was as fat behind, sir, as he was before.
This ram was ten miles high, sir. Indeed he may be more.

The teeth that were in his mouth, sir, were like a regiment of men.
And the tongue that hung between them, sir, would have fed them twice again.
The butchers that slew this ram, sir, were near-drowned in the blood
And the boys that held the pails, sir, were carried away in the flood.

The tanners that tanned his hide, sir, were never again poor,
For when they had tanned and stretched it, sir, it reached to Sinfin Moor.
The tail was a hundred yards, sir, as near as I could tell.
'Twas sent off to Rome, sir, to ring St. Peter's bell.

All the women of Derbyshire, sir, came begging for his ears,
To make them leather aprons, sir, to last them forty years.
It took all the boys of Derby, sir, to carry away his bones
And all the girls of Derby, sir, to roll away his stones.

The mutton that the ram gave, sir, gave the British army meat,
And what was left, I'm told, sir, was given to the fleet.
Now if you won't believe me, sir, or think I tell a lie,
Just ask the folks in Derby, sir. They're as trustworthy as I.

DO YOUR EARS HANG LOW?

Do your ears hang low? Do they wobble to and fro?
Can you tie them in a knot? Can you tie them in a bow?
Can you toss them o'er your shoulders like the continental soldiers?
Do you ears hang low? Yes, my ears hang low. They wobble to and fro.

I can tie them in a knot. I can tie them in a bow.
I can toss them o'er my shoulder like a continental soldier.
Yes, my ears hang low. Yes, our ears hang low. They wobble to and fro.

We can tie them in a knot. We can tie them in a bow.
We can toss them o'er our shoulders, 'cause we're continental soldier.
Yes, our ears hang low!

ESAU AND THE SEESAW

When I saw Esau and saw what he saw, then I saw Esau and saw the seesaw.
He saw the seesaw and saw me see him see the seesaw standing by the sea.
I saw that he saw me see what he saw, the seaside seesaw, the sea and Esau.
Then I saw Esau sit on the seesaw. Soon on the seesaw me sitting he saw.

So me and Esau did see and seesaw. So did we seesaw the seesaw we saw.
When I left that sea and the sea's seesaw, 'twas the last I'd see seesawing Esau.
Another like Esau never would I see, none like he I saw that day by the sea.
If a lone Esau and seesaw you see, sit on the seesaw and seesaw for me.

THE FARMER's IN THE DELL

The farmer's in the dell. The farmer's in the dell.
Heigh-ho, the dairy-o! The farmer's in the dell.
The farmer takes a wife. The farmer takes a wife.

Heigh-ho, the dairy-o! The farmer takes a wife.

The wife takes a child. The wife takes a child.
Heigh-ho, the dairy-o! The wife takes a child.
The child takes a nurse. The child takes a nurse.
Heigh-ho, the dairy-o! The child takes a nurse.

The nurse takes a dog. The nurse takes a dog.
Heigh-ho, the dairy-o! The nurse takes a dog.
The dog takes a cat. The dog takes a cat.
Heigh-ho, the dairy-o! The dog takes a cat.

The cat takes a rat. The cat takes a rat.
Heigh-ho, the dairy-o! The rat takes the cheese.
The cheese stands alone. The cheese stands alone.
Heigh-ho, the dairy-o! The cheese stands alone.

FATHER CAME FROM PARIS
Father came from Paris. Mother came from York.
I ate with a spoon before I used a fork. Brother came before me, sister afterward.
I made noises before I her words heard.
Brother calls me, "brother". Sister does so too. I counted before she came up to two.
Father dotes on mother; grandma dotes on sis. I now get food in my mouth and don't miss.
Ice cream is my favorite. Spinach I don't like. I give what's baddest to my dog named Tyke.

GOD BLESS MY UNDERWEAR
God bless my underwear, my only pair. Stand beside them, and guide them,
Through the rips, through the holes, through the tears.
From the washer, to the dryer, to my backpack, to my rear.
God bless my underwear, my only pair. God bless my underwear, or I'd be bare.

GOOBER PEAS
Sitting by the roadside on a summer's day,
Chatting with my mess-mates, passing time away,
Lying in the shadows underneath the trees --
Goodness how delicious! -- eating goober peas,
Peas, peas, peas, peas, eating goober peas --
Goodness how delicious! -- eating goober peas.

When a horse-man passes, the soldiers have a rule

To cry out their loudest, "Mister, where's your mule?",
But another custom, enchantinger than these
Is wearing out your grinders, eating goober peas.

Just before the battle, the General hears a row.
He says "The Yanks are coming, I hear their rifles now."
He looks down the roadway and what d'you think he sees?
The Georgia Militia cracking goober peas.

I think my song has lasted just about enough.
he subject's interesting, but the rhymes are mighty rough.
I wish the war was over so free from rags and fleas
We'd kiss our wives and sweethearts, and eat our goober peas.

GO TELL AUNT RHODY

Go tell Aunt Rhody, go tell Aunt Rhody,
Go tell Aunt Rhody: "The old gray goose is dead,
The one she's been saving, the one she's been saving,
The one she's been saving to make a feather bed.

She died in the millpond. She died in the millpond.
She died in the millpond a-standing on her head.
The old gander's weeping. The old gander's weeping.
The old gander's weeping because his wife is dead.

The goslings are mourning. The goslings are mourning.
The goslings are mourning because they're mother's dead.
We'll grind her into sausages. We'll grind her into sausages.
We'll grind her into sausages to feed to Uncle Ted.

We'll pluck her goose feathers. We'll pluck her goose feathers.
We'll pluck her goose feathers to make a feather bed.

THE GREEN GRASS GREW

There once was a tree, a pretty little tree,the prettiest little tree that you ever did see.
Oh, the tree in a hole and the hole in the ground
And the green grass grew all around, all around and the green grass grew all around.

Now on this tree there was a limb, the prettiest little limb that you ever did see
Oh, the limb on the tree and the tree in a hole and the hole in the ground ...

Now on this limb there was a branch, the prettiest little branch that you ever did see.
Oh, the branch on the limb and ...

Now on this branch there was a bough, the prettiest little bough that you ever did see.
Oh, the bough on the branch and ...

Now on this bough there was a twig, the prettiest little twig that you ever did see.
Oh, the twig on the bough and ...

Now on this twig there was a leaf, the prettiest little leaf, that you ever did see.
Oh, the leaf on the twig and ...

GREAT GREEN GOBS OF GREASY GRIMY GOPHER GUTS
Great, green gobs of greasy, grimy gopher guts,
Marinated monkey brains, little, dirty birdies' feet,
Great, green gobs of greasy, grimy gopher guts,
And I forgot my spoon!

One-quart cans of all-purpose porpoise pus,
Old, moldy goober nuts, monkey vomit, camel snot,
One-quart cans of all-purpose porpoise pus,
And I forgot my spoon!

French-fried eyeballs floating in a bowl of blood,
Vulture vomit at my feet, chewed-up parakeet,
French-fried eyeballs floating in a bowl of blood,
And I forgot my spoon!

THE GYPSY ROVER
The gypsy rover came over the hill down through the valley so shady.
He whistled and he sang 'til the green wood rang
And he won the heart of a lady. Adido, adido daday, adido, adidaydi.
He whistled and he sang 'til the green wood rang and he won the heart of a lady.

She left her father's castle gate. She left her own fond lover.
She left her servants and estate to follow the gypsy rover.
Adido, adido daday, adido, adidaydi.
He whistled and he sang 'til the green wood rang and he won the heart of a lady.

Her father saddled up his fastest steed. He roamed the valley all over
And sought his daughter at great speed and the whistling gypsy rover.
Adido, adido daday, adido, adidaydi.
He whistled and he sang 'til the green wood rang and he won the heart of a lady.

He came at last to a mansion fine down by the river Clady
And there was music and there was wine for the gypsy and the lady.
Adido, adido daday, adido, adidaydi.
He whistled and he sang 'til the green wood rang and he won the heart of a lady.

"He is no gypsy, my father," she said. "But lord of these lands all over
And I will stay 'til my dying day with my whistling 'gypsy rover'."

HELL'S TOO HOT

Hell's Too hot! Hell's too hot! Hell's too hot for me!
The demons go there. They can stay there. Hell's to hot for me.
Hell's too hot for me. Hell's too hot for me.
You can go there if you want to. Hell's too hot for me,
Very hot, much too hot, way too hot for me!

Hell's Too hot! Hell's too hot! Hell's too hot for me!
I am trusting in my Savior. Hell's too hot for me.
Hell's too hot for me. Hell's too hot for me.
Jesus went there, didn't stay there. Hell's too hot for me,
Very hot, much too hot, way too hot for me!

Hell's Too hot! Hell's too hot! Hell's too hot for me!
I am going on to Heaven. Hell's too hot for me.
Hell's too hot for me. Hell's too hot for me.
I'll not go where God is not there. Hell's too hot for me,
Very hot, much too hot, way too hot for me!

THE HEPHALUMPH

Well, I went to hunt the hephalumph in the land of Wildersmere
And if you do not know the place, I'll tell you where it's near.
It's not too close to Fleeglestown and farther still from Glarf,
But you'll know you're near to Wildersmere when you hear the hephalumph snarf.

The hephalumph's snarf is horrible and quite deafening as well,
But the spoor of this beastie's worse, like something spewed from hell.

It stinks worse than vomit or skunk and sticks to shoes like glue,
And may I be a bingo if my story 'tisn't true!

The hephalumph's tracks are hard to miss as you'd expect from its size,
But when it's quiet as a mouse, it's snarf's a big surprise, a sudden and thunderous roar
when you're without a clue, and may I be a bingo if my story 'tisn't true!

The hephalumph can smell quite well and knows when you approach
And though it sees very poorly, could crush you like a roach.
So look both ways, to right and left, and back and forward too,
And may I be a bingo if my story 'tisn't true!

Oh, the hephalumph is fourteen feet when measured from ear to ear
And though he has but three of them, he rightly cannot hear.
His nose is red. His eye is green. His tail is turquoise blue,
And may I be a bingo if my story 'tisn't true!

Now though I've told you all about the wondrous hephalumph,
You do not seem to believe me. I'll not be made a chump,
So we'll have to find a way Wildersmere go back to
And may we both be bingoes if our story 'tisn't true.

HERE WE GO ROUND THE MULBERRY BUSH
Here we go round the mulberry bush, The mulberry bush, the mulberry bush.
Here we go round the mulberry bush on a cold and frosty morning.
This is the way we wash our hands, wash our hands, wash our hands.
This is the way we wash our hands on a cold and frosty morning.

This is the way we go to school, go to school, go to school.
This is the way we go to school on a cold and frosty morning.
This is the way we come back home, come back home, come back home.
This is the way we come back home on a cold and frosty morning.

HE's A PEACH OF A SAVIOR
He's a **peach** of a Savior. He's the **apple** of my eye.
He **prunes** back the branches when the branches grow too high,
He bears **fruit** in season and His love will never die
And that's why I'm **bananas** for the Lord!
Glory! Glory! We're the branches!
Glory! Glory! We're the branches!

And that's why I'm **bananas** for the Lord!

I wouldn't give a **fig** to hear what the **grape**vine has to say,
'Cause I know I know that He, Who sin did take away,
Heals every wound **or in**jury's coming back to stay ...

His depths I could never **plum**b. He is great beyond com**pare**,
Beyond comprehending and yet always ever there.
My cross helping **bear, He** does my every sorrow share ...

Heaven's **key we** have from Him and eternal life sub**lime**
He's every sin removed far beyond all space and time,
Every prob**lem on** Earth, every error, flaw or crime ...

He'll be **raisin'** up the dead, but I'll just have to wait.
My **current** plan's simply with His to co-operate,
Because He has revealed just the Father knows the **date** ...

HICKORY DICKORY DOCK
Hickory, dickory, dock, the mouse ran up the clock.
The clock struck struck one. The mouse ran down. Hickory, dickory dock.
... The clock struck two. The mouse ran through.
... The clock struck three. The mouse ruan free.
... The clock struck four. It ran on the floor.
... The clock struck five. The mouse is alive.
... The clock struck six. The mouse named Mick's.
... The clock struck eight. The mouse just ate.
... The clock struck nine. The mouse will dine.
... The clock struck ten. It ran in the den.

HUSH, LITTLE BABY
Hush, little baby. Don't you cry. Mama's going to buy you a mockingbird.
If that mockingbird won't sing, Mama's going to buy you a diamond ring.
If that diamond ring turns brass, Mama's going to buy you a looking glass.
If that looking glass gets broke, Mama's going to buy you a billy goat.

If that billy goat won't pull, Mama's going to buy you a cart and bull.
If that cart and bull turns over, Mama's going to buy you a dog named Rover.
If that dog named Rover won't bark, Mama's going to buy you a horse and cart.
If that horse and cart fall down, You'll still be the prettiest girl in town.

I GAVE MY LOVE A CHERRY

I gave my love a cherry that has no stone.
I gave my love a chicken that has no bone.
I gave my love a story that has no end.
I gave my love a baby with no cryin'

.

How can there be a cherry that has no stone?
How can there be a chicken that has no bone?
How can there be a story that has no end?
How can there be a baby with no cryin'?

A cherry when it's bloomin' has no stone.
A chicken when it's pippin' has no bone.
The story that I love her has no end.
A baby when it's sleepin' has no cryin'.

I HAD A ROOSTER

I had a rooster and the rooster pleased me. I fed my rooster 'neath a greenberry tree,
The little rooster went "Cock-a-doodle-doo, dee doodle-dee, doodle-dee doo!"

I had a cat and the cat pleased me. I fed my cat 'neath a greenberry tree.
The little cat went "Meow! Meow!". The little rooster went …

I had a pig and the pig pleased me. I fed my pig 'neath a greenberry tree.
The little pig went "Oink! Oink! Oink!" The little cat went …

I had a cow and the cow pleased me. I fed the cow 'neath a greenberry tree.
The little cow went "Moo! Moo! Moo!" The little pig went …

I had a duck and the duck pleased me. I fed my duck 'neath a green berry tree.
The little duck went "Quack! Quack! Quack!" The little cow went …

I had a lion and the lion pleased me. I fed my lion 'neath a greenberry tree.
The little lion went "Roar! Roar!" The little duck went …

I had a baby and the baby pleased me. I fed my baby 'neath a greenberry tree.
The little baby went "Waa! Waa! Waa!" The little lion went …

I'M MY OWN GRANDPA

It sounds funny I know, but it really is so. O, I'm my own grandpa.
I'm my own grandpa. I'm my own grandpa.

It sounds funny I know, but it really is so. O, I'm my own grandpa.

Now many, many years ago when I was 23,
I was married to a widow who was pretty as could be.
This widow had a grown-up daughter who had hair of red.
My father fell in love with her and soon they too were wed.

This made my dad my son-in-law and changed my very life
For my daughter was my mother, 'cause she was my father's wife.
To complicate the matter, even though it brought me joy,
I soon became the father of a bouncing baby boy.

My little baby then became a brother-in-law to dad,
And so became my uncle, though it made me very sad,
For, if he was my uncle, then that also made him brother
Of the widow's grown-up daughter who, of course, was my step-mother.

Father's wife then had a son who kept them on the run,
And he became my grandchild for he was my daughter's son.
My wife is now my mother's mother and it makes me blue,
Because, although she is my wife, she's my grandmother too.

Now, if my wife is my grandmother, then I'm her grandchild
And every time I think of it, it nearly drives me wild,
For now I have become the strangest case you ever saw
As husband of my grandmother, I'm my own grandpa.

JACK AND JILL
Jack and Jill went up the hill to fetch a pail of water.
Jack fell down and broke his crown and Jill came tumbling after.
Up Jack got and home did trot as fast as he could caper,
Went to bed to mend his head with vinegar and brown paper.

Jill came in and she did grin to see his paper plaster.
Mother, vexed, did scold her next for laughing at Jack's disaster.
So the two did resolve to from then on to be wary
And to choose never to lose the water they might carry.

JOHN JACOB JINGLEHEIMER SCHMIDT
John Jacob Jingleheimer Schmidt, his name is my name too!

Whenever we go out the people always shout:
"There goes John Jacob Jingleheimer Schmidt! Ja! Ja! Ja! Ja! Ja! Ja! Ja!"

John Jacob Jingleheimer Schmidt, father and son are we!
Whenever we go out the people always shout:
"There goes John Jacob Jingleheimer Schmidt! Ja! Ja! Ja! Ja! Ja! Ja! Ja!"

John Jacob Jingleheimer Schmidt, Junior's my son's name!
Whenever we go out the people always shout:
"There goes John Jacob Jingleheimer Schmidt! Ja! Ja! Ja! Ja! Ja! Ja! Ja!"

John Jacob Jingleheimer Schmidt, Senior's my dad's name!
Whenever we go out the people always shout:
"There goes John Jacob Jingleheimer Schmidt! Ja! Ja! Ja! Ja! Ja! Ja! Ja!"

LITTLE SQUIRRELY
Little squirrely up the tree, I see you. Do you see me?
I will climb into your tree very improbably.
Little bunny in the hole, I'll not make your home my goal.
I'm no danger; I'm no troll, not a weasel or a mole.

Little snakie in the grass, I'll move aside so you can pass.
I'll show respect and never sass and won't today you harass.
Little gnatie in the air, I almost didn't see you there.
I'm glad I saw you flying there and not feel you inside somewhere.

Little cloudie floating by, you make me wonder, make me sigh.
"Why" I wonder, "cannot I float like you way up high?"
Little antie on the ground, I see you crawling around,
Making no noise, not a sound, seeking whate'er can be found.

Little kitty on my lap, I see you're taking a catnap.
Though you purr, I won't clap, won't spread my legs, make a gap.
Little fishie in the stream, bright you are with golden gleam.
I won't catch you. I won't scream; I might wake up from this dream.

LONDON BRIDGE
London bridge is falling down, falling down, falling down!
London bridge is falling down, my fair lady.
Build it up with sticks and stones, sticks and stones, sticks and stones.

Build it up with sticks and stones, my fair lady.

Build it up with needles and pins,
needles and pins, needles and pins.
Build it up with needle and pins, my fair lady.

Build it up with iron bars, iron bars, iron bars.
Build it up with iron bars, my fair lady.

MARY HAD A LITTLE DOG
Mary had a little dog, little dog, little dog.
Mary had a little dog that chewed trees in the park
And when its newborn puppies came, puppies came, puppies came,
And when its newborn puppies came, each one was full of bark.

Mary had a little cat, little cat, little cat, Mary had a little cat that had great big paws,
When Santa down the chimney comes, chimney comes, chimney comes,
When Santa down the chimney comes, it poor old Santa claws.

Mary had a little pig, little pig, little pig, Mary had a little pig who big ones would take on,
And after it was through with them, through with them, through with them,
And after it was through with them, she'd bring home the bacon.
Mary had a little bird, little bird, little bird.
Mary had a little bird with the sweetest song she'd heard.
And when Mary passed the field, passed the field, passed the field,
And when Mary passed the field so too'd the farmer's herd.

MICHAEL FINNEGAN
There once was a man named Michael Finnegan. He grew whiskers on his chinnegan.,
Shaved them off and they grewinnegan. Poor old Michael Finnegan. (Beginnegan!)
There once was a man named Michael Finnegan. He got drunk from too much ginnegan.
So in the street he fellinnegan. Poor old Michael Finnegan. (Beginnegan!)

There once was a man named Michael Finnegan, Thought he'd never see his kinnegan,
But sobered up the morninginnegan. Poor old Michael Finnegan. (Beginnegan!)
There once was a man named Michael Finnegan. Who played poker thinking he'd winnegan,
But his last dollar he putinagen. Poor old Michael Finnegan. (Beginnegan!)

There once was a man named Michael Finnegan. He kicked up an awful dinnegan., 'Cause he
was told he must not sinnegan. Poor old Michael Finnegan. (Beginnegan!)

There once was a man named Michael Finnegan. He went fishing with a pinnegan,
Caught a fish but dropped itinnegan. Poor old Michael Finnegan. (Beginnegan!)

There once was a man named Michael Finnegan, Climbed a tree and scraped his shinnegan,
Took off several yards of skinnegan. Poor old Michael Finnegan. (Beginnegan!)
There once was a man named Michael Finnegan. He grew fat and then grew thinnegan,
Then he died, so he can't beginnegan. Poor old Michael Finnegan.

MINDMELDER's LAMENT
When I started thinking when I was just a tot
I learned to think of thinking and not to think of not,
But much of the thoughts I've thought I think I can rethink not,
Still there's a certain thought I think I think that I cannot not:

"I thought I thought I thought a thought, but only thought I did.
That thought that I thought I thought was not that thought I thought I thought I did.
"'Twas a thought I'd never thought and yet now I think I did!"

When I think I've thought that thought more than I think I ought,
I try to think of nothing rather than think that thought,
But then that unthought thought that I'd thought that I'd forgot
Proves it's one I can't not think and in my thoughts I've got:

MIRACLE MIKE
Miracle Mike the chicken didn't have a head,
Which wouldn't be a miracle, except he wasn't dead.
When he had his head cut off it wasn't very nice.
One small ear, a smaller brain had now to suffice.

Miracle Mike the chicken traveled all around.
For a quarter for a peek better wasn't found.
He made the tour of sideshows, circuses and fairs,
But no other of the freaks to our Mike compares.

In eighteen months Mike fin'lly died in a motel,
Choked to death on his spittle, but there's more to tell.
The farmer who had chopped him and hoped to rich get
Only enough money got to get out of debt.

THE OLD FAMILY TOOTHBRUSH

The old family toothbrush, that dirty old toothbrush,
That slimy, old toothbrush that hangs on the wall.
O, first it was father's and then it was mother's
And then it was sister's and now it is mine.
O, father misused it and mother abused it
And sister refused it and now it is mine!

OLD MACDONALD

Old MacDonald had a farm, E-I-E-I-O!, and on this farm he had some chicks, E-I-E-I-O!,
With a "Chick! Chick!" here and a "Chick! Chick!" there,
Here a "Chick!", there a "Chick!", everywhere a "Chick! Chick!".
Old MacDonald had a farm, E-I-E-I-O!

... And on this farm he had some turkeys, E-I-E-I-O!,
With a "Gooble! Gooble!" here and a "Gooble! Gooble!" there,
Here a "Gooble!", there a "Gooble!", everywhere a "Gooble! Gooble!".

... And on this farm he had some sheep, E-I-E-I-O!,
With a "Baa! Baa!" here and a "Baa! Baa!" there,
Here a "Baa!", there a "Baa!", everywhere a "Baa! Baa!".

And on this farm he had some cows, E-I-E-I-O!,
With a "Moo! Moo!" here and a "Moo! Moo!" there, Here a "Moo!", there a "Moo!", everywhere
a "Moo! Moo!".

And on this farm he had some pigs, E-I-E-I-O!,
With a "Oink! Oink!" here and a "Oink! Oink!" there,
Here a "Oink!", there a "Oink!", everywhere a "Oink! Oink!".

And on this farm he had some ducks, E-I-E-I-O!,
With a "Quack! Quack!" here and a "Quack! Quack!" there,
Here a "Quack!", there a "Quack!", everywhere a Quaick! Quack!".

ON TOP OF MY PIZZA

On top of my pizza all covered with sauce
I could find no mushrooms. I think they got lost.
I looked in the closet. I looked in the sink.
I looked in the cup that held my soft drink.

I looked under the table and the tablecloth.
I even looked into my root beer's froth.
I looked under my plate and my neighbor's too
And soon was wond'tring "What more can I do?"

I went to kitchen and talked to the cook.
He said "They're not here, but you can look."
I looked on the floor and the ceiling too,
But only found pepperoni-mozzarella goo.

I looked in the saucepan right under the lid.
Wherever I looked those mushrooms stayed hid.
I called the police who wouldn't help me,
Unless they'd been taken by a cat up a tree.

I called the coast guard, marines and navy,
Air force, secret service and the army.
On mushrooms on pizza I finally gave up.
Now only on mushroom soup do I sup.

ON TOP OF SPAGHETTI
On top of spaghetti all cover with cheese
I lost my last meatball when somebody sneezed.
It rolled off the table and onto the floor
And that my poor meatball rolled out of the door.

It rolled off the front porch and down the first step,
Then on the second, I could swear it leapt.
It sped down the sidewalk without slowing down,
But hitting the curb turned it around.

Right through the garage into the back yard
My poor, little meatball was taking it hard.
Now it was misshapened and discolored too,
And very soon my meatball'd be through.

It rolled out into garden and under a bush,
By then my poor meatball was nothing but mush
The mush was as tasty as tasty could be,
And then the next summer, it grew into a tree.

The tree was all covered, all covered with moss
And on it grew meatballs and tomato sauce.
So take care when you're eating spaghetti with cheese,
You may loose your meatball, if someone should sneeze.

But if you are lucky, lucky like me,
Your meatball will become a meatball tree,
Then you will never be without a meatball,
For you will harvest them every Fall.

O, THERE AIN'T NO BUGS ON ME

O, there ain't no bugs on me (on me). There ain't no bugs on me.
There may be bugs on some of you mugs, but there ain't no bugs on me.
O, there ain't no flies on me (on me). There ain't no flies on me.
There may be flies on some of you guys, but there ain't no flies on me.

O, mosquito he fly high (fly high) and mosquito he fly low.
If old mosquito lands on me, He ain't a gonna fly no mo'.
Well little bugs have littler bugs. Up on their backs to bite'em
And the littler bugs have still littler bugs and so ad infinitum.

Some people say that fleas are black, but I know that ain't so,
'Cause Mary had a little lamb Whose fleas was white as snow.

THE OTHER DAY

The other day (the other day) I met a bear (I met a bear)
Up in the woods (up in the woods) away up there (away up there).
The other day I met a bear, up in the woods away up there .

He looked at me. (He looked at me.) I looked at him. (I looked at him.)
He sized up me. I sized up him. He looked at me, I looked at him.
He sized up me, I sized up him. He said to me (he said to me) "Why don't you run?
I see you ain't (I see you ain't) got any gun (got any gun)",
He said to me "Why don't you run? I see you ain't got any gun." And so I ran (and so I ran)
away from there (away from there), And right behind (and right behind)
Me was that bear (me was that bear), And so I ran away from there,
and right behind me was that bear,
And then a tree (and then a tree) that I did spy (that I did spy), Whose lowest branch
(whose lowest branch)

Was ten feet high (was ten feet high) And then a tree that I did spy:
its lowest branch was ten feet high,
And so I leapt (and so I leapt)
into the air (into the air) And missed that branch (and missed that branch)
Away up there (away up there),
And so I leapt into the air,
and missed that branch away up there.
Now, don't you fret (now don't you fret)
And don't you frown (and don't you frown) I caught that branch (I caught that branch)
Second time round (second time round), Now, don't you fret and don't you frown.
I caught that branch second time round.
So that's the end (so that's the end).
There ain't no more (there ain't no more), 'Cause I don't go ('cause I don't go)
there any more (there any more), So that's the end. There ain't no more!

POLLY WOLLY DOODLE
O, I went down South for to see my Sal, singing "Polly Wolly Doodle" all the day.
My Sal she is a spunky gal, singing "Polly Wolly Doodle" all the day.
Fare thee well, fare thee well, fare thee well, my fairy fay,
For I'm going to Louisiana for to see my Suzianna, singing "Polly Wolly Doodle" all the day.

O, my Sal she is a maiden fair, singing "Poly Wolly Doodle" all the day,
With curly eyes and laughing hair, singing "Polly Wolly Doodle" all the day.
O, a grasshopper sitting on a railroad track, singing "Polly Wolly Doodle" all the day,
A-picking his teeth with a carpet tack, singing "Polly Wolly Doodle" all the day.

O, I went to bed, but it wasn't no use, singing "Polly Wolly Doodle" all day,
My feet stuck out like a chicken roost, singing "Polly Wolly Doodle" all day.
Behind the barn down on my knees, singing "Polly Wolly Doodle" all day.
I thought I heard a chicken sneeze, singing "Polly Wolly Doodle" all day.

He sneeze so hard with the whooping cough, singing "Polly Wolly Doodle" all day,
He sneeze his head and tail right off, singing "Polly Wolly Doodle" all day.

POP GOES THE WEASEL
All around the cobbler's bench, the monkey chased the weasel.
The monkey thought 'twas all in fun. Pop goes the weasel!
Johnny's got the whooping cough and Mary's got the measles.
That's the way the money goes. Pop goes the weasel!

A penny for a spool of thread, a penny for a needle.
That's the way the money goes. Pop goes the weasel!
You may try to sew and sew and never make anything regal,
So roll it up, let it go. Pop goes the weasel!

A painter would his lover paint. He stood before the easel.
The monkey jumped all o'er his paint. Pop goes the weasel!
When his sweetheart did laugh, his temper got so lethal,
He tore the painting up in half. Pop goes the weasel!

My son and I went to the fair. We saw a lot of people.
We spent a lot of money there. Pop goes the weasel!
I got sick from all the sun. Sonny boy got the measles.
Even so we had lots of fun. Pop goes the weasel!

I climbed up and down the coast to find a golden eagle.
I climbed the rocks, thought I was close. Pop goes the weasel!
But, alas, I lost my way, saw nothing but a seagull.
I tore my pants, wasted the day. Pop goes the weasel!

I went to the grocery store. I thought a little cheese'll
Help to catch a mouse in the house. Pop goes the weasel!
But the mouse was very bright, wasn't a mouse to wheedle.
It took the cheese and said, "Goodnight!" Pop goes the weasel!

If you want to buy a pig, buy you a pig with hair on,
One that's a penny for every pair on. Pop goes the weasel!
I haven't time to sit and sigh, waste no time to tease'll.
So kiss me quick. Bye! I'm off. Pop goes the weasel!

A SAILOR WENT TO SEA

A sailor went to sea, sea, sea to see what he could see, see, see.
But all that he could see, see, see was the bottom of the deep, blue sea, sea, sea.
The sailor came o'er here, here, here to hear what he could hear, hear, hear,
But all that he could hear, hear, hear was the sound of the surf in his ear, ear, ear.

The sailor went o'er there, there, there to see who was there, there, there,
But all that he found there, there, there was that they're there there.
The sailor rode a steamboat, boat, boat. The steamboat had a bell, bell, bell
And when he went to heaven; the steamboat went to

The bottom of the deep, blue sea, sea, sea.

THE SAVE OUR TONGUE SOCIETY SONG

Save our tongue! Save our tongue! Save our tongue! Save our tongue!
He Who was to rise indeed rose, But not every prize is prose,
A grammatical surprise's surprose.

Save our tongue! Save our tongue! Save our tongue! Save our tongue!
Save Our Tongue Society, Save Our Tongue Society,
Save Our Tongue Society, save our tongue!

One more than no men is man, but more than no hen's not han,
More than one wren is not wran.
With your fingers you can feel felt, but you could never steal stelt,
Or a elephant seal selt.

A boy who swims will soon have swum, but milk that's skimmed is seldom skum,
The nails you trim cannot be trum.
Any bird that did fly flew. No liar that did lie ever lew,
Nor buyer that did buy ever bew.

When words you speak those words are spoken, but a nose tweaked's not twoken
And what you seek's not often soken.
Did you hear the stampede I heard, but not fear the stampede I feard,
Yet steered the stampede I steard?

Couples who mate must have met, but even if they ate they've not et,
Or while on a date didn't det.
If we forget, then we've forgotten, but things that are wet are not wotten
And houses let cannot be lotten.

More than one goose is geese, but never were moose meese,
Neither were nooses neese.
The plural of mouse is mice, but house's is houses not hice,
And souse's souses not sice.

Every light needs to be lit, but no blight is ever blit,
Nor ever a dark night nit.
In the field were many oxen, in the dryer socks not soxen,
In this book knock-knocks not knock-knoxen.

The creeper to the window crept, though a peeper he didn't pept,
When his beeper didn't bept.
This book that Rainbeau wrote has been written, but the fight he didn't fight wasn't fitten,
And the rite he didn't right wasn't ritten.

The goods one sells are always sold, but fears dispelled are not dispold
And when you smell you're not smold.
Everything that's been given God gave, but not even He wiven wave,
Or could any siven save.

A wound, if not stopped, bleeds blood, but a steed is not often a stood,
Not a need often a nood.
When young you oft a top saw spun, but did you see a grin e'er grun?
Or a potato neatly skun?

SHE'LL BE COMING

She'll be coming round the mountain when she comes.
She'll be coming round the mountain when she comes.
She'll be coming round the mountain. She'll be coming round the mountain.
She'll be coming round the mountain. She'll be coming round the mountain when she comes.

She'll be driving six white horses when she comes.
She'll be driving six white horses when she comes.
She'll be driving six white horses. She'll be driving six white horses.
She'll be driving six white horses. She'll be driving six white horses when she comes.

O, we'll all go out to meet her when she comes.
O, we'll all go out to meet her when she comes.
O, we'll all go out to meet her. O, we'll all go out to meet her.
O, we'll all go out to meet her. O, we'll all go out to meet her when she comes.

And we'll all have chicken and dumplings when she comes,
And we'll all have chicken and dumplings when she comes,
And we'll all have chicken and dumplings.
We'll all have chicken and dumplings when she comes,
We'll all have chicken and dumplings. We'll all have chicken and dumplings when she comes.

SKIP TO MY LOU

Lou, Lou, skip to my Lou, Lou, Lou, skip to Lou,

Lou, Lou, skip to my Lou, Skip to my Lou, my darling.
Lost my partner, what'll I do? Lost my partner what'll I do?
Lost my partner, what'll I do? Skip to my Lou, my darling.

I'll find another one prettier than you. I'll find another one prettier than you.
I'll find another one prettier than you. Skip to my Lou, my darling.

Little red wagon painted blue, little red wagon painted blue,
Little red wagon painted blue. Skip to my Lou, my darling.
Can't get a redbird, a bluebird'll do, Can't get a redbird, a bluebird'll do,
Can't get a redbird, a bluebird'll do. Skip to my Lou, my darling.

Cows in the meadow moo, moo, moo, Cows in the meadow moo, moo, moo,
Cows in the meadow moo, moo, moo. Skip to my Lou, my darling.
Flies in the buttermilk! Shoo, shoo, shoo! Flies in the buttermilk! Shoo, shoo, shoo!
Flies in the buttermilk! Shoo, shoo, shoo! Skip to my Lou, my darling.

THE SLITHERY D
The slithery D slipped out of the sea. It got all the others, but it won't get me.
The slithery D got the captain and mate. The slithery D both of them ate.
The slithery D got passengers and crew. It got all the others, but won't get me too.
The slithery D is getting quite near. The slithery D will soon be here.
O, you won't get me, you slither D. You got all the others, but you won't get ....

THE SONG THAT NEVER ENDS
This is "The Song That Never Ends". It just goes on and on, my friends,
Some people started singing it, not knowing what it was. Now they'll just keep on singing it
forever just because ...

TEN LITTLE INDIANS
One little, two little, three little Indians, four little five little, six little Indians,
Seven little, eight little nine little Indians, ten little Indian boys.

Ten little, nine little, eight little Indians, seven little, six little, five little Indians,
Four little, three little, two little Indians, one little Indian boy.

One little, two little, three little Indians, four little, five little, six little Indians,
Seven little, eight little nine little Indians, ten little Indian girls.

Ten little, nine little, eight little Indians, seven little, six little, five little Indians,

Four little, three little, two little Indians, one little Indian girl.

Two little, two little, two little Indians, two little, two little, two little Indians,
Two little, two little, two little Indians, one Indian boy and girl.

THERE WAS A BEE-EYE-EE-EYE-EE
There was a bee-eye-ee-eye-ee sat on a wall-eye-all-eye-all
And there he sat-eye-at-eye-at and that was all-eye-all-eye-all.
Then came a boy-eye-oy-eye-oy who had a stick-eye-ick-eye-ick
And gave that bee-eye-ee-eye-ee an awful lick-eye-ick-eye-ick,

And so that boy-eye-oy-eye-oy let out a yell-eye-ell-eye-ell
And told that bee-eye-ee-eye-ee to go someplace I will not tell
And then that bee-eye-ee-eye-ee gave one big cough-eye-ough-eye-ough
And one last smile-eye-ile-eye-ile and he buzzed off-eye-off-eye-off.

THERE WERE THREE JOLLY FISHERMEN
There were three jolly fishermen. There were three jolly fisherman,
Fisher, fishermen, men, men, fisher, fishermen, men, men.
There were three jolly fishermen.

The first one's name was Abraham. The first one's name was Abraham,
Abra, Abraham ham, ham, Abra, Abraham ham, ham.
The first one's name was Abraham.

The next one's name was Isaac. The next one's name was Isaac.
I, Isaac, Zack, Zack, I, Isaac, Zack, Zack.
The next one's name was Isaac.

The last one's name was Jacob. The last one's name was Jacob,
Jac, Jacob cob, cob, Jac, Jacob cob, cob.
 The last one's name was Jacob.

They all sailed up to Jericho. They all sailed up to Jericho,
Jeri, Jericho cocoa, Jeri, Jericho cocoa.
They all sailed up to Jericho.

They didn't go to Timbuktu. They didn't go to Timbuktu,
Timbuk, Timbuktu tutu. Timbuk, Timbuktu tutu.
They didn't go to Timbuktu.

They didn't go to Calcutta. They didn't go to Calcutta.
Calcutt, Calcutta, ta-ta, Calcutt, Calcutta, ta-ta.
They didn't go to Calcutta.

They didn't go to Tokyo. They didn't go to Tokyo.
Toky, Tokyo yo-yo, Toky, Tokyo yo-yo.
They didn't go to Tokyo.

They didn't go to Washington. They didn't go to Washington.
Washing, Washington ton, ton, Washing, Washington ton, ton.
They didn't go to Washington.

They didn't go to Istanbul. They didn't go to Istanbul,
Istan, Istan, bul, bul, bul, Istan, Istanbul bull, bull.
They didn't go to Istanbul.

They didn't go to Katmandu. They didn't go to Katmandu.
Katman, Katmandu doo-doo, Katman, Katmandu ...

They didn't go to Amsterdam.
They didn't go to Amsterdam, Amster, Amster...

THERE'S A HOLE IN THE BOTTOM OF THE SEA
There's a hole in the bottom of the sea.
There's a hole in the bottom of the sea. There's a hole. There's a hole.
There's a hole. There's a hole. There's a hole in the bottom of the sea.
There's a log in the hole in the bottom of the sea.
There's a log in the hole in the bottom of the sea.
There's a log. There's a log. There's a log. There's a log.
There's a log in the hole in the bottom of the sea.

There's a branch on the log in the hole in the bottom of the sea,
There's a branch on the log in the hole in the bottom of the sea,
There's a branch. There's a branch. There's a branch. There's a branch.
There's a branch on the log in the hole in the bottom of the sea.

There's a bump on the branch on the log in the hole in the bottom of the sea.
There's a bump on the branch on the log in the hole in the bottom of the sea.
There's a bump. There's a bump. There's a bump. There's a bump.

There's a bump on the branch on the log in the hole in the bottom of the sea.

There's a frog on the bump on the branch on the log in the hole in the bottom of the sea.
There's a frog on the bump on the branch on the log in the hole in the bottom of the sea.
There's a frog. There's a frog. There's a frog. There's a frog.
There's a frog on the bump on the branch on the log in the hole in the bottom of the sea.

There's a tail on the frog on the bump on the branch
on the log in the hole in the bottom of the sea.
There's a tail on the frog on the bump on the branch
on the log in the hole in the bottom of the sea.
There's a tail. there's a tail. There's a tail. there's a tail.
There's a tail on the frog on the bump on the branch
on the log in the hole in the bottom of the sea.

There's a speck on the tail on the frog on the bump On the branch on the log
in the hole in the bottom of the sea. There's a speck on the tail on the frog on the bump
On the branch on the log in the hole in the bottom of the sea.
There's a speck. There's a speck. There's a speck on the tail
On the frog on the bump on the branch on the log in the hole in the bottom of the sea.

There's a fleck on the speck on the tail on the frog on the bump on the branch
on the log in the hole in the bottom of the sea.
There's a fleck on the speck on the tail on the frog on the bump on the branch
on the log in the hole in the bottom of the sea.
There's a fleck. There's a fleck. There's a fleck on the speck on the tail
on the frog on the bump on the branch on the log in the hole in the bottom of the sea.

THERE'S A HOLE IN THE BUCKET
There's hole in the bucket, dear Liza, dear Liza.
There's a hole in the bucket, dear Liza, a hole.
Then mend it, dear Henry, dear Henry, dear Henry.
Then mend it, dear Henry. Dear Henry, mend it.

With what shall I mend it, dear Liza, dear Liza?
With what shall I mend it, dear Liza, with what?
With straw, dear Henry, dear Henry, dear Henry,
With straw, dear Henry, dear Henry, with straw.

The straw is too long, dear Liza, dear Liza.
The straw is too long, dear Liza, too long.

Then cut it, dear Henry, dear Henry, dear Henry.
Then cut it, dear Henry. Dear Henry, cut it.

With what shall I cut it, dear Liza, dear Liza?
With what shall I cut it, dear Liza, with what?
With a knife, dear Henry, dear Henry, dear Henry,
With a knife, dear Henry, dear Henry, a knife.

The knife is too dull, dear Liza, dear Liza.
The knife is too dull, dear Liza, too dull.
Then sharpen it, dear Henry, dear Henry, dear Henry.
Then sharpen it, dear, Henry. Dear Henry, sharpen it.

With what shall I sharpen it, dear Liza, dear, Liza?
With what shall I sharpen it, dear Liza, with what?
With a stone, dear Henry, dear Henry, dear Henry,
With a stone, dear Henry, dear Henry, a stone.

The stone is too dry, dear Liza, dear Liza.
The stone is too dry, dear Liza, too dry.
Then wet it, dear Henry, dear Henry, dear Henry.
Then wet it, dear Henry. Dear Henry, wet it.

With what shall I wet it, dear Liza, dear Liza?
With what shall I wet it, dear Liza, with what?
With water, dear Henry, dear Henry, dear Henry,
With water, dear Henry, dear Henry, water.
In what shall I fetch it dear Liza, dear Liza?
In what shall I fetch it, dear Liza, it what?
In a bucket, dear Henry, dear Henry, dear Henry,
In a bucket, dear Henry, dear Henry, bucket.

THE HOUSE THAT JACK BUILT
This is the house that Jack built.
This is the malt that lay in the house that Jack built.
This is the rat, that ate the malt that lay in the house that Jack built.
This is the cat, that killed the rat, that ate the malt that lay in the house that Jack built.

This is the dog, that worried the cat, that killed the rat,
That ate the malt that lay in the house that Jack built.

This is the cow with the crumpled horn, that tossed the dog, that worried the cat,
That killed the rat, that ate the malt that lay in the house that Jack built.

This is the maiden all forlorn, that milked the cow with the crumpled horn,
That tossed the dog, that worried the cat, that killed the rat,
That ate the malt that lay in the house that Jack built.

This is the man all tattered and torn, that kissed the maiden all forlorn,
That milked the cow with the crumpled horn, that tossed the dog, that worried the cat,
That killed the rat, that ate the malt that lay in the house that Jack built.

This is the priest all shaven and shorn, that married the man all tattered and torn,
That kissed the maiden all forlorn, that milked the cow with the crumpled horn,
That tossed the dog, that worried the cat, that killed the rat,
That ate the malt that lay in the house that Jack built.

This is the cock that crowed in the morn, that waked the priest all shaven and shorn,
That married the man all tattered and torn, that kissed the maiden all forlorn,
That milked the cow with the crumpled horn, that tossed the dog, that worried the cat,
That killed the rat, that ate the malt that lay in the house that Jack built.

This is the farmer sowing his corn, that kept the cock that crowed in the morn,
That waked the priest all shaven and shorn, that married the man all tattered and torn,
That kissed the maiden all forlorn, that milked the cow with the crumpled horn,
That tossed the dog, that worried the cat, that killed the rat,
That ate the malt that lay in the house that Jack built.

THE THING

While I was walking down the beach one bright and sunny day,
I saw a great big wooden box afloating in the bay.
I pulled it in and opened it up and much to my surprise
Oh, I discovered a [clap, clap, clap] right before my eyes.
Oh, I discovered a [clap, clap, clap] right before my eyes.

I picked it up and ran to town as happy as a king.
I took it to a guy I knew who'd buy most anything,
But this is what he hollered at me as I walked into his shop:
"Oh, get out of here with that [clap, clap, clap] before I call a cop!
Oh, get out of here with that [clap, clap, clap] before I call a cop!"

I turned around and got right out, running for my life
And then took it home with me to give it to my wife,
But this is what she hollered at me as I walked in the door:
"Oh, get out of here with that [clap, clap, clap] and don't come back no more!
Oh, get out of here with that [clap, clap, clap] and don't come back no more!"

I wandered all around the town until I chanced to meet,
A hobo who was looking for a handout on the street,
He said he'd take most anything. He was a desperate man,
But, when I showed him the [clap, clap, clap] he turned around and ran.
Oh, when I showed him the [clap, clap, clap] he turned around and ran.

I wandered on for many years a victim of my fate.
Until, one day, I came upon St. Peter at the gate
And when I tried to take it inside, he told me where to go:
"Get out of here with that [clap, clap, clap] and take it down below!
Oh, get out of here with that [clap, clap, clap] and take it down below!"

The moral of this story is if you're out on the beach,
And you should see a great big box, and it's within your reach,
Don't ever stop and open it up, that's my advice to you,
'Cause you'll never get rid of that [clap, clap, clap] no matter what you do.
No, you'll never get rid of that [clap, clap, clap] no matter what you do.

THIS OLD MAN
This old man, he played one. He played knick-knack on my thumb.
With a knick-knack paddywhack, give the dog a bone, this old man came rolling home.
This old man, he played two. He played knick-knack on my shoe.
With a knick-knack paddywhack, give the dog a bone, this old man came rolling home.

This old man, he played three. He played knick-knack on my knee.
With a knick-knack paddywhack, give the dog a bone, this old man came rolling home.
This old man, he played four. He played knick-knack on my floor.
With a knick-knack paddywhack, give the dog a bone, this old man came rolling home.

This old man, he played five. He played knick-knack while alive.
With a knick-knack paddywhack, give the dog a bone, this old man came rolling home.
This old man, he played six. He played knick-knack just for kicks.
With a knick-knack paddywhack, give the dog a bone, this old man came rolling home.

This old man, he played seven. He played knick-knack up to heaven.
With a knick-knack paddywhack, give the dog a bone, this old man came rolling home.
This old man, he played eight. He played knick-knack at the gate.
With a knick-knack paddywhack, give the dog a bone, this old man came rolling home.

This old man, he played nine. He played knick-knack one more time.
With a knick-knack paddywhack, give the dog a bone, this old man came rolling home.
This old man, he played ten. He played knick-knack yet again.
With a knick-knack paddywhack, give the dog a bone this old man came rolling home.

THIS SONG HAS JUST EIGHT WORDS

Has this song just eight words? Has this song just eight words?
Has this song just eight words? Just eight words this song has.
This song has just eight words. This song has just eight words.
This song has just eight words, the just just this, the Word!

Has this song the word "has"? Has this song the word "has"?
Has this song the word "has"? The word, "has", this song has.
This song has the word, "has",This song has the word, "has",
This song has the word, "has", the just just this, the Word!

Has this song just eight words? Has this song just eight words?
Has this song just eight words? Just eight words this song has.
This song has just eight words. This song has just eight words.
This song has just eight words, the just just this, the Word!

Has this song the word "this"? Has this song the word "this"?
Has this song the word "this"? The word, "this", this song has.
The word, "this", this song has. The word, "this", this song has.
This song has the word, "this", the just just this, the Word!

Has this song the word "song"? Has this song the word "song"?
Has this song the word "song"? The word, "song", this song has.
The word, "song", this song has. The word, "song", this song has.
This song has the word, "song", the just just this, the Word!

Has this song the word "has"? Has this song the word "has"?
Has this song the word "has"? The word, "has", this song has.
The word, "has", this song has. The word, "has", this song has.
This song has the word, "has", the just just this, the Word!

Has this song the word "just"? Has this song the word "just"?
Has this song the word "just"? The word, "just", this song has.
The word, "just", this song has. The word, "just", this song has.
This song has the word, "just", the just just this, the Word!

Has this song the word "eight"? Has this song the word "eight"?
Has this song the word "eight"? The word, "eight", this song has.
The word, "eight", this song has. The word, "eight", this song has.
This song has the word, "eight", the just just this, the Word!

Has this song the word "words"? Has this song the word "words"?
Has this song the word "words"? The word, "words", this song has.
The word, "words", this song has. The word, "words", this song has.
This song has the word, "words", the just just this, the Word!

Has this song the word "the"? Has this song the word "the"?
Has this song the word "the"? The word, "the", this song has.
The word, "the", this song has. The word, "the", this song has.
This song has the word, "the", the just just this, the Word!

Has this song the word "word"? Has this song the word "word"?
The word, "word", this song has. The word, "word", this song has.
The word, "word", this song has. The word, "word", this song has.
This song has the word, "word", the just just this, the Word!

TIE ME KANGAROO DOWN

Tie me kangaroo down, Brown. Tie me kangaroo down.
Tie me kangaroo down, Brown. Tie me kangaroo down.

Play your digeridoo, Lou. Play your digeridoo.
Keep playin' 'til you're through, Lou. Play your digeridoo.
Watch me wallaby's feed, Reed. Watch me wallaby's feed.
They're a finicky breed, Reed, so watch me wallabies feed.

Let me wombats go loose, Bruce. Let me wombats go loose.
They're of no further use, Bruce, so let me wombats go lose.
Take me koala bear back, Jack. Take me koala bear back.
It lived somewhere out on the track, Jack, so take me koala bear back.

Mind me platypus duckbill. Mind me platypus duck.
Don't let him go runnin' amuck, Bill, just mind me platypus duck.
Tan me roo's hide when I'm dead, Fred. Tan me roo's hide when I'm dead.
So we tanned his hide, when he died, Clyde, and that's it hangin' on the shed.

TUTU
Tutu was a racehorse and Won-one was one too.
When Tutu raced with Won-one how did the duo do?
Tutu tied with Won-one, since their races numbered two,
And though Won-one won one Tutu won one too.

WHEN NOAH SAILED
When Noah sailed the waters blue,
He had troubles worse than you.
'Twas more than a year on that ark
Before he found a place to park.
Then he found a mountain high
A place his bird found dry,
So Noah and all could disembark,
Because that dove was no meadow lark.

WOULDN'T IT BE BETTER?
Wouldn't it be better if birds flew in the sky?
If they used their wings to soar both low and high?
If they flew up in the air and not bulls and cows?
When one landed on your head, you'd have smaller ows.

Wouldn't it be better if fish swam in the sea?
O, just think of how much better it would be!
Instead of hunting for them underneath the ground,
Beneath the waves or ice is where they would be found.

Wouldn't it be better if things fell down, not up?
Your hot chocolate wouldn't fly out of your cup.
Then your hat would sit on and warm your chilly head
And you wouldn't have to sleep underneath your bed.

Wouldn't it be better if stars shone in the night

And the day was lit with only sunny light?
Then it could rise at dawn and set down in the West.
O wouldn't it be better? Wouldn't it be best?

Wouldn't it be better if we did not have war,
If no one used any weapons any more?
O wouldn't it be better? Wouldn't it be great?
If everyone learned to love and no longer hate?

www.ingramcontent.com/pod-product-compliance
Lightning Source LLC
Chambersburg PA
CBHW071832020426
42331CB00007B/1698